Pocket Guide
ROCKS
& MINERALS

DAVID COOK & WENDY KIRK

LAROUSSE

Key to coloured tabs

The rocks and minerals in this book are arranged into the groups listed below. Minerals are traditionally grouped on the basis of their chemical composition, distinguishing, for example, native elements from oxides or silicates. The rocks are arranged into three groups, as igneous, metamorphic or sedimentary. Use the colour tab on the corner of the pages to find a particular group as you flick through the book.

Native elements

Sulphides

Oxides

Halides

Carbonates

Sulphates

Tungstate

Phosphates

Silicates

Igneous rocks

Metamorphic rocks

Sedimentary rocks

Larousse plc
Elsley House, 24-30 Great Titchfield Street,
London W1P 7AD

This edition published by Larousse 1995
10 9 8 7 6 5 4 3

This edition © Larousse plc 1995
Text copyright © David Cook and Wendy Kirk
and Grisewood and Dempsey Ltd 1991
Illustrations copyright © Grisewood and
Dempsey 1991
Material in this edition was first published by
Kingfisher in *Field Guide to Rocks and Minerals of
the World* 1991

BRITISH LIBRARY CATALOGUING-IN-PUBLICATION DATA
A catalogue record for this book is available
from the British Library

ISBN 0 7523 0009 1

Senior Editor: Michèle Byam
Assistant Editor: Mandy Cleeve
Design: Smiljka Surla

Colour separations: Friendly Graphics, Hong Kong
Printed in Hong Kong

Contents

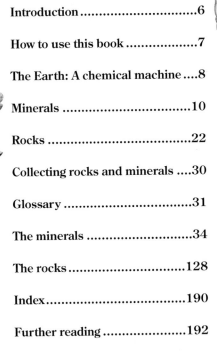

Introduction

Since the earliest times, people have been fascinated by rocks and minerals. Part of the attraction lies in their economic importance. Indeed the terms Stone Age, Bronze Age and Iron Age indicate periods of history when the uses of these materials were discovered and exploited. Since the onset of the Iron Age, materials from the Earth's crust have been used in myriad ways. Stones, bricks, sand and cement are used in buildings and roads, and iron and steel in engineering. Aviation, ceramics, electronics and metal coating are among the many modern industries that utilize the Earth's mineral resources.

Apart from their uses, many rocks and minerals are attractive in appearance and are sought by eager collectors. The worth of many specimens, including precious stones and metals, is enhanced by special features, such as hardness, brilliance, durability or scarcity. For example, its rarity, appearance and resistance to discolouration gives gold a unique place in international commerce. Other materials, throughout history, have had magical or curative properties ascribed to them.

Minerals and rocks have long given pleasure to many people, both professionals and amateurs. Their study has also enabled us to locate important resources such as oil, and has led to improved techniques for extracting many materials. Several aspects of these sciences, such as crystallography and the dating of rocks, have been established for some time. On the other hand we are gaining new insights into processes that operate inside the Earth. The revolutionary theory of plate tectonics, was established only in the 1960s and is still developing. By studying such processes, scientists are able to unravel further the fascinating story of the history of the Earth.

GEOLOGICAL TIME SCALE		
Era	Period	Time (millions of years ago)
Cenozoic	Quaternary	2
	Tertiary	65
Mesozoic	Cretaceous	145
	Jurassic	208
	Triassic	245
Paleozoic	Permian	290
	Carboniferous	362
	Devonian	408
	Silurian	439
	Ordovician	510
	Cambrian	570
Precambrian		

HOW TO USE THIS BOOK

The introduction to this book gives a general overview of the subject of rocks and minerals, dealing with their formation, occurrence, and the qualities to note when making an identification. Many of the technical terms used by geologists to describe minerals and rocks are also explained, including definitions of the headings found in the fact panel. Further definitions can be found in the Glossary on pages 31–33. Because of the technical nature of the subject, it is worth familiarizing yourself with these concepts before consulting the individual entries.

Each page is devoted to a different species, and contains some explanatory text, with photographs of examples of different forms of the rock or mineral concerned. In the case of some minerals, line drawings illustrate the crystal structure or cleavage patterns. A fact panel summarizes the main features, against which you can check any specimen you have found. The most important identifying features of minerals are asterisked.

The colour shows which group of rocks or minerals each entry belongs to, for quick reference. The colour code is explained on page 2.

A text summarizes the main features of a rock or mineral and describes any notable varieties. Information is given about uses, famous localities and the origin of names.

Typical examples are illustrated with photographs. Line drawings in some entries illustrate specific features such as crystal form.

Labels point out important features for identification.

A fact panel includes detailed information about the properties of the species. Asterisks denote the most important distinguishing features of minerals. Examples are provided of large deposits or particularly fine specimens.

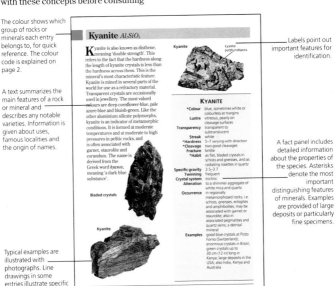

Kyanite Al_2SiO_5

Kyanite is also known as disthene. This refers to the fact that the hardness along the length of kyanite crystals is less than the hardness across them. This is the mineral's most characteristic feature. Kyanite is mined in several parts of the world for use as a refractory material. Transparent crystals are occasionally used in jewellery. The most valued colours are deep cornflower-blue, pale azure-blue and bluish-green. Like the other aluminium silicate polymorphs, kyanite is an indicator of metamorphic conditions. It is formed at moderate temperatures and at moderate to high pressures in pelitic rocks, and is often associated with garnet, staurolite and corundum. The name is derived from the Greek word *kyanos*, meaning 'a dark blue substance'.

Bladed crystals

Kyanite

Kyanite

kyanite porphyroblasts

KYANITE

*Colour	blue, sometimes white or colourless at margins
Lustre	vitreous, pearly on cleavage surfaces
Transparency	transparent to subtranslucent
Streak	white
*Hardness	5–7 varying with direction
*Cleavage	two good cleavages
*Fracture	brittle
*Habit	as flat, bladed crystals in schists and gneisses, and as radiating rosettes in quartz
Specific gravity	3.5–3.7
Twinning	frequent
Crystal system	triclinic
Alteration	to a shimmer aggregate of white mica and quartz
Occurrence	in regionally metamorphosed rocks, i.e. schists, gneisses, eclogites and amphibolites; may be associated with garnet or staurolite; also in associated pegmatites and quartz veins; a detrital mineral
Examples	good blue crystals at Pizzo Forno (Switzerland); enormous crystals in Brazil; green crystals up to 30 cm (12 in) long in Kenya; large deposits in the USA; also India, Kenya and Australia

94

THE EARTH: A CHEMICAL MACHINE

In order to study rocks and minerals it is useful to know something of the Earth's composition and formation. The Earth as a whole has a particular chemical constitution but within it are a wide range of rocks and minerals of diverse chemical make-up. Minerals may be scarce, occurring as small grains, or may occur in high concentrations, sometimes of economic importance. Rocks vary from dull, soft clays to hard, bright, crystalline granites. What then are the forces that have formed the Earth and its major chemical components?

The Earth consists of an extremely dense core, a fairly dense mantle and a relatively thin light crust. The core itself consists of a liquid outer layer and a solid inner layer. Gravity, a major force that shapes the Earth, has concentrated heavy materials such as iron and its sulphides into the core, while light magnesium and aluminium silicates dominate in the crust.

Heat is important in shaping the Earth. Heat creates the large-scale convection currents in the mantle which help to move large slabs of crust and upper mantle, known as *plates*, around the surface of the Earth. New plate material is produced at *constructive plate margins*, usually ocean ridges. The plates move apart at a rate of 2–18cm (0.8–7.2in) per year. This is balanced, however, by the loss of material at *destructive plate margins*. Here plates move into the mantle down *subduction*

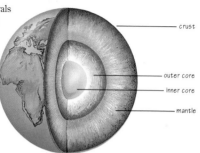

Beneath the Earth's thin crust are the mantle and the core. The inner core is solid but the outer core is fluid.

zones where they melt to form magma.

Most of our knowledge of rocks and minerals is of those in the Earth's crust; relatively little is known about the composition of the mantle and core. But it is thought that the upper mantle may contain such heavy rocks as peridotite, which appears occasionally on the

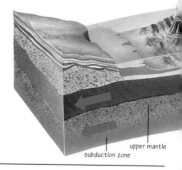

surface, but is heavier than most crustal rocks. This guide describes many of the rocks and minerals in the crust and the processes that formed them.

What are minerals and rocks?

First, we can define the terms rocks and minerals. Minerals are naturally occurring, inorganic (lifeless) substances. Coal, oil and natural gas are not minerals, because they are mixtures of organic chemicals formed from once-living matter. They are usually called fossil fuels. Minerals consist of elements, substances that cannot be broken down into other substances by chemical

means. Some minerals, called the *native elements* consist of only one element, for example platinum or gold. However, most are chemical combinations of two or more elements (see page 18). Each mineral has a definite composition and any part of a mineral is much the same as any other part. Rocks are composed of mineral grains, but the proportions of minerals vary from one sample to another. Sometimes, as in limestone, a rock is composed mostly of one mineral, but most rocks consist of a number of different minerals.

The diagram shows oceanic crust being produced at an ocean ridge. New rock is formed from magma rising from the mantle. It is carried from the ridge on a moving plate of upper mantle. The plate is then forced downwards beneath a plate margin of continental crust. Rocks on the descending plate melt. The molten material rises and forms intrusions and volcanoes.

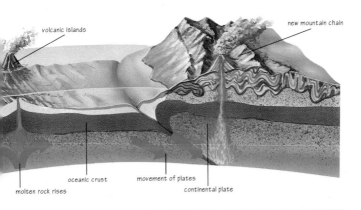

volcanic islands

new mountain chain

molten rock rises

oceanic crust

movement of plates

continental plate

MINERALS

Minerals are the building blocks that make up rocks. Scientists describe minerals as naturally occurring, inorganic substances. Nearly all minerals have a definite atomic structure that gives them a characteristic crystal shape. The study of minerals is the oldest branch of Earth science. For example, the recognition and use of copper probably dates back to 6000 BC. Collecting minerals has become a very popular hobby, and this field guide describes the properties used to identify minerals. This is often not easy, and requires careful observation using a hand lens, and lots of practice. A few simple chemical tests are given, but great care must be taken when using these. The most useful features for identifying each mineral are given an asterisk (*) in the main text.

Colour

This is the most familiar property of minerals, but is often not the most useful, because many minerals show a variety of colours depending on the impurities they contain. For example, quartz may be colourless, white, pink, yellow, mauve, blue or black. Some minerals nearly always have the same colour due to their chemical composition. Here, colour can be useful in identification. For example, sulphur is bright yellow, malachite is always green, azurite is always blue. These minerals are said to be *idiochromatic*, as opposed to minerals of variable colour, which are said to be *allochromatic*.

Streak

More consistent and reliable than a mineral's colour is the colour of its streak (the mineral in powdered form). The streak is consistent regardless of colour variation in different specimens. It is usually produced by scratching the mineral across a piece of unglazed porcelain, or by crushing a small portion. A penknife may also be used to scratch the surface and produce a powder. Idiochromatic minerals usually have a streak which is slightly lighter than the colour of the specimen. Allochromatic minerals generally have a white or greyish white streak. However, some minerals show a streak which contrasts with the colour of the mineral. For example, the pale gold mineral pyrite has a yellowish black streak, while grey-black hematite produces a cherry-red one. Streak is rarely a diagnostic property of the silicate minerals. These are often too hard to produce a streak, and it is usually white.

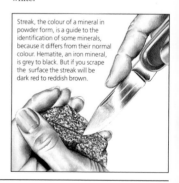

Streak, the colour of a mineral in powder form, is a guide to the identification of some minerals, because it differs from their normal colour. Hematite, an iron mineral, is grey to black. But if you scrape the surface the streak will be dark red to reddish brown.

Lustre

This refers to the amount and quality of reflected light coming from the surface of the mineral. It may be *metallic* or *non-metallic*. A metallic lustre is produced by opaque minerals that absorb a lot of light. This is the lustre of metals and is also shown by many sulphides, such as chalcopyrite. A less perfect metallic lustre, known as *sub-metallic*, is shown by some of the semi-opaque oxides, such as hematite. A non-metallic lustre is shown by transparent and translucent minerals. It includes a variety of types, as defined below:

Adamantine a high degree of sparkle, as shown by diamond.

Vitreous the lustre of broken glass, as in quartz and many of the silicates. (Calcite shows a sub-vitreous lustre.)

Resinous the lustre of resin, as in amber, opal and some varieties of sphalerite.

Pearly the lustre of a pearl, caused by the reflection of light from a series of parallel surfaces within a crystal. It is shown by talc and cleavage faces of selenite (gypsum).

Silky the lustre of silk. This is confined to minerals that have a fibrous structure, such as satin spar, a variety of gypsum.

Greasy this is produced in minerals with tiny irregularities on the surface, such as nepheline.

Earthy minerals that do not show a lustre are said to be earthy or dull.

Transparency

Mineralogists usually indicate the transparency of minerals – that is, whether the mineral is *transparent*, *translucent*, or *opaque*. But these terms are rarely of value in mineral identification. The degree of transparency depends to a large extent on how thick the specimen is, and also on the presence of inclusions (fragments of other substances within the specimen), cleavage planes and any internal flaws.

metallic lustre

silky lustre

resinous lustre

Introduction

Hardness

Hardness is a measure of the resistance of a mineral to scratching or abrasion. It is given as a number between 1 and 10 according to a reference set of minerals set up by the Austrian mineralogist Friedrich Mohs in 1812. Number 1 is the softest and number 10 is the hardest. Each mineral can scratch any with a lower number, but can be scratched only by those with a higher number.

The hardness of a mineral is determined by finding which minerals in Mohs' scale scratch it, and which it will scratch. It is best to use a hand lens, as a

softer mineral may leave a powder trail when scraped along a harder mineral, giving the false impression of a scratch. Where these minerals are not available, the test can be carried out using a fingernail (hardness 2–2.5), a copper coin (hardness 3) or a steel knife-blade (hardness 5.5–6.5). Minerals with a hardness over 6 will scratch glass.

Cleavage

Many minerals tend to break along sets of well-defined planes, which are related to the internal arrangement of the atoms. This property is known as *cleavage*, and a mineral may break in one or more directions. For example, mica shows a good cleavage in one direction, readily splitting into thin sheets. This is because the bonding between atoms within the sheets is much stronger than the bonding between the sheets. This type of cleavage is known as *basal cleavage*. Cleavage is related to the crystal system to which a mineral belongs (see the section on 'Crystal systems' below). Galena, which crystallizes in the cubic system, shows an excellent cleavage in three directions parallel to the faces of a cube. Fluorite, which also crystallizes in the cubic system, shows octahedral cleavage – that is the cleavage is parallel to the faces of an octahedron. Other directions commonly encountered are parallel to prism faces, pyramid faces, or the faces of a rhombohedron. Some specimens may show surfaces known as *partings*, which are superficially similar to, but more widely spaced than cleavage planes. They are different in origin from cleavage and are not present in all specimens of any one mineral.

MOHS' SCALE

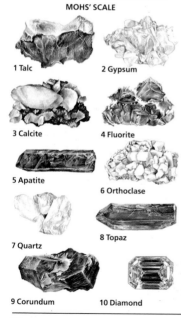

1 Talc

2 Gypsum

3 Calcite

4 Fluorite

5 Apatite

6 Orthoclase

7 Quartz

8 Topaz

9 Corundum

10 Diamond

Fracture

This term refers to the shape of the broken surface of the mineral, as opposed to the cleavage surface and is occasionally of use in identification. Terms used to describe fracture are as follows:

Conchoidal fracture is the most distinctive, and is that shown by broken glass. The mineral breaks with a concave or convex surface, which often shows concentric ridges looking rather like growth lines on a shell. It is shown by quartz and olivine.

Even the fracture surface is flattish, as in garnet.

Uneven most minerals show this kind of fracture, where the surface is characterized by minute elevations and depressions.

Hackly the fracture surface is covered with small, jagged points, as in native copper.

Tenacity

This property is included with fracture in this guide. Tenacity refers to the way minerals react to shock, crushing, cutting and bending. Terms used are as follows:

Sectile the mineral can be cut with a knife, and the slice breaks up under a hammer, as in graphite.

Malleable a slice from the mineral will flatten when hammered, as in native copper.

Flexible thin sheets of the mineral will bend, as in talc.

Elastic the bent portion will spring back when pressure is released. For example, mica flakes are flexible and elastic, whereas talc and molybdenite are flexible but inelastic.

Brittle most minerals are brittle, and will crumble when hit, as in iron pyrites and fluorspar.

rhombohedral cleavage

basal cleavage

conchoidal fracture

Introduction

Specific gravity

Although rarely determined accurately, specific gravity may be a useful property whenever a specimen feels lighter or heavier than 'normal'. Specific gravity is the ratio of the weight of a body to that of an equal volume of water. Most minerals and rocks show a specific gravity of between 2.5 and 3. With practice, the specific gravity of an unknown mineral can be estimated; where this departs from the normal range, it is usually on the high side. The relationship between colour and specific gravity may be helpful, because dark minerals are often relatively heavy, whereas light coloured minerals are often relatively light. Exceptions to this rule can therefore be identified fairly easily. For example, baryte, a white mineral, appears surprisingly heavy (specific gravity=4.5), whereas dark grey graphite feels light (specific gravity=2.23). Examples of other minerals with a high specific gravity are the ore minerals galena (7.5), pyrite (5.0) and chalcopyrite (4.2).

Alteration

After a mineral is formed, various conditions may cause it to change or alter to other minerals. Common alteration processes are weathering and hydrothermal activity. Alteration products can be a good clue to the identity of the original mineral, especially those that have characteristic colours.

Other features

Some minerals have unusual properties that may be useful in identification. Some of these characteristics are given in the right-hand column:

Magnetism magnetite is the only common mineral which is strongly magnetic. This property distinguishes it from chromite.

Taste halite (rock salt) and sylvite can be distinguished by their taste. Sylvite tastes like rock salt, but is more bitter.

Odour a few minerals can be identified by their smell when hit, rubbed or heated. For example, when pyrite is struck it gives off a smell of burning sulphur. When arsenic compounds are heated, they give off a smell of garlic.

Fluorescence some minerals glow in the dark when exposed to ultraviolet light or X-rays. This is known as *fluorescence*, after the mineral fluorite, which illustrates this property well.

Phosphorescence minerals which glow in the dark for a time after being exposed to light are called *phosphorescent*.

Piezoelectricity and pyroelectricity when some minerals are stressed, they acquire an electric charge. This is described as a *piezoelectric effect*. Quartz, which has this property, is frequently used in electrical equipment and in radio receivers and transmitters. Other minerals become charged when heated. It has long been known that tourmaline, when heated in the embers of a fire, first attracts and then repels the ashes. This is known as *pyroelectricity*.

Radioactivity certain elements are *radioactive*, emitting radiation which can be detected using a Geiger counter. This property is shown by pitchblende, which is the main ore of uranium.

CRYSTALS

Most minerals, if allowed to grow unrestricted, will form crystals. Crystals are more or less symmetrical solids bounded by flat (or *planar*) faces. The crystal shape reflects the internal arrangement of the atoms, which pack together in a regular three-dimensional framework. The best crystals are formed by slow, uninterrupted growth. Some minerals readily form large, well shaped crystals, whereas others do so only rarely. The study of crystals may be useful in identifying certain minerals, such as garnet and pyrites, as they form particular shapes.

Habit and form

The set of faces produced by the symmetry of the crystal is known as the *form*. Crystals of the same mineral may look very different, as a single mineral may show more than one form. For example, pyrite has both cubic and octahedral crystals.

If the form totally encloses a space, as in a cube, it is said to be *closed*. If not, it is said to be *open*. An example of this is a prism, which is not closed at the ends. Open forms must always be combined with other forms.

The form commonly taken by single crystals is described in this guide under the heading 'Habit'. Some minerals do not form crystals at all, but are *amorphous*, forming structureless masses.

Habit refers to the appearance of single crystals or crystalline *aggregates* that do not show perfect crystal shapes. In a crystal, some faces may grow better than others. For example, a mineral may show well developed prism faces, so that it is much longer in one direction than the other two. Its habit is then described as *prismatic*. Other terms are:

Acicular fine, needle-shaped crystals, as in rutile.

Bladed flattened like a knife-blade, as in kyanite.

Botryoidal like a bunch of grapes, as in chalcedony.

Dendritic branching tree-like or moss-like, as in native copper.

Fibrous fine, thread-like strands, as in asbestos.

Mammilated round and mutually interfering masses, as in malachite; the protuberances are larger and more flattened than botryoidal.

Massive crystalline aggregates with no regular form.

Radiating radial crystals or fibres, as in nodular pyrite.

Reniform kidney-shaped, as in hematite.

Tabular showing broad, flat surfaces, as in baryte.

Introduction

Crystal systems

Crystals may be grouped together into seven systems based on their symmetry. Crystals may show one or more planes and/or axes of symmetry, and may have a centre of symmetry. A plane of symmetry can be illustrated using a matchbox. There are three ways in which this can be cut into two parts, so that one half is the mirror image of the other. Thus it shows three planes of symmetry.

The matchbox also shows three lines or axes of symmetry, each passing through the centres of two opposite faces, so that when it is rotated once about each axis, the same view appears twice. Thus the matchbox is said to show three *axes* of *two-fold rotation*. Similarly, crystals may show axes of *three-*, *four-*, or *six-fold rotation*. The matchbox, and many crystals, has a centre of symmetry, as each face on one side has a corresponding parallel face on the other.

Each crystal system is defined by the number and types of symmetry elements present. To each system are assigned reference axes, which determine the orientation of the crystal faces. In most crystal systems, the reference axes lie along the axes of symmetry. The angles between them vary from system to system. The characteristics of each system are summarized in the table opposite. Examples of crystal forms in each system are illustrated.

The regular shapes of the crystals shown here may not be so apparent in real specimens. This is because some crystal faces may grow larger than others, and their shape is altered. However, the angle between any two particular faces is always the same for all crystals of the same mineral.

Crystal systems

Crystals that belong to the cubic crystal system must all have 4 three-fold axes of symmetry. There are 3 reference axes, a_1, a_2 and a_3. They are all right angles to each other and are of equal length.

Crystals of the tetragonal crystals system are characterized by the presence of a single vertical axis of four-fold symmetry. There are 3 reference axes, c, differs in length from the horizontal axes, a_1 and a_2.

The orthorhombic crystal system is characterized by 3 perpendicular two-fold axes of symmetry, or 1 two-fold axis at the intersection of two perpendicular planes of symmetry. The 3 reference axes, a, b and c, are at right angles to each other, but are of different lengths.

Monoclinic crystals must contain 1 two-fold axis of symmetry. The reference axes, a, b and c, are of different lengths. The vertical axis, c, is not at right angles to axis a. The symmetry axis, b, is at right angles to the plane containing the other two.

Crystals of the triclinic system have either no symmetry or just a centre of symmetry. There are 3 reference axes, a, b and c, of different lengths, none of which are at right angles to each other.

The hexagonal system has 1 vertical six-fold axis of symmetry, while the trigonal system has a three-fold one. They have the same reference axes, The three horizontal ones, a_1, a_2 and a_3, are equal in length and at an angle of 120 to each other. The vertical axis, c, differs in length to the other three.

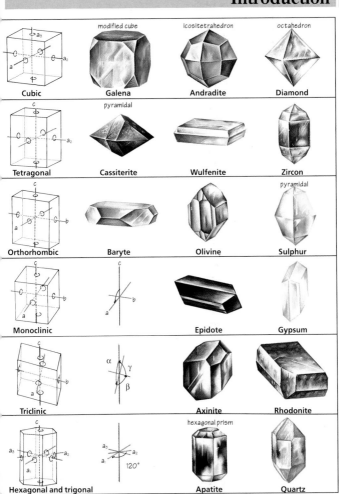

Cubic	Galena (modified cube)	Andradite (icositetrahedron)	Diamond (octahedron)
Tetragonal	Cassiterite (pyramidal)	Wulfenite	Zircon
Orthorhombic	Baryte	Olivine	Sulphur (pyramidal)
Monoclinic		Epidote	Gypsum
Triclinic		Axinite	Rhodonite
Hexagonal and trigonal		Apatite (hexagonal prism)	Quartz

Introduction

Twinning

A twinned crystal is made up of two or more parts. One part of the crystal is in a reversed orientation to the adjacent part. Twins are recognized by the presence of *re-entrant* angles (angles that point inwards).

Twinning can occur simply by contact across a flat surface, forming *contact twins*, such as in rutile. In other cases, the twin cannot be divided into two separate halves, rather the halves appear to have grown through each other. These are known as *interpenetrant twins*, as

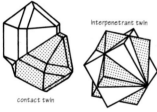

Interpenetrant twin

contact twin

seen in fluorite. Twins may be single or repeated (*polysynthetic*), as in albite.

CHEMISTRY OF MINERALS

Each mineral has a distinctive chemical composition, which may be fixed, or may vary within certain limits. This composition is expressed as a chemical formula. Some minerals, known as the *native elements*, contain only one element. Most minerals, however, are compounds containing more than one element. They comprise two charged parts called *ions*. The negatively charged *anions* often contain oxygen. The symbols for the elements used in this pocket guide are given below, together with the names and formulas of common anions referred to.

An example of a simple mineral formula is NaCl, the formula for halite, or sodium chloride. It contains one sodium atom and one chlorine atom per molecule. A slightly more complicated

Symbols for Elements				Common Anionic Groups	
Ag	Silver	Li	Lithium	Al_2O_4	Aluminate
Al	Aluminium	Mg	Magnesium	As	Arsenide
As	Arsenic	Mn	Manganese	AsO_4	Arsenate
Au	Gold	Mo	Molybdenum	Bo_3	Borate
B	Boron	Na	Sodium	Cl	Chloride
Ba	Barium	O	Oxygen	Co_3	Carbonate
Be	Beryllium	P	Phosphorous	CrO_4	Chromate
Bi	Bismuth	Pb	Lead	F	Fluoride
C	Carbon	Pt	Platinum	MoO_4	Molybdate
Ca	Calcium	S	Sulphur	N	Nitride
Cl	Chlorine	Sb	Antimony	NO_3	Nitrate
Co	Cobalt	Si	Silicon	O	Oxide
Cr	Chromium	Sn	Tin	OH	Hydroxide
Cu	Copper	Sr	Strontium	PO_4	Phosphate
F	Flurine	Ti	Titanium	S	Sulphide
Fe	Iron	U	Uranium	SiO_4	Silicate
H	Hydrogen	W	Tungsten	SO_4	Sulphate
Hg	Mercury	Zn	Zinc	TiO_3	Titanate
K	Potassium	Zr	Zirconium	WO_4	Tungstate

formula is that for calcite, $CaCO_3$, or rutile, TiO_2. The numbers refer to the number of atoms of the preceding element that are present in one molecule of the mineral. Sometimes minerals form chemical series. An example of this is the olivine series, written as $(Mg,Fe)SiO_4$. This means that atoms of magnesium and iron can substitute for one another, to form a continuously variable series from a pure magnesium olivine to a pure iron olivine.

Chemical tests

Some simple chemical tests are helpful in identifying minerals. In particular, geologists carry dilute hydrochloric acid (HCl) in the field. If a drop is placed on calcite, it will effervesce (fizz, giving off gas), whereas quartz does not react. This is one way in which the two superficially similar minerals can be distinguished. Dolomite, another carbonate mineral like calcite, also reacts, but the reaction is much slower. Great care must be taken even when using dilute acids to avoid contact with skin and clothes, and to avoid breathing in fumes.

Where laboratory facilities are available, other chemical tests can be carried out, such as for solubility in acids. A powdered sample of the mineral is placed in acid in a test-tube and, if required, is gently warmed. Flame colouration tests are carried out by holding a chip of mineral in a flame with a pair of forceps. The hottest part of the flame is used, at the tip of the blue cone. The colour of the flame indicates which element is present. For example, a green flame indicates baryte, which contains barium.

FIELD OCCURRENCE OF MINERALS

All rocks are made up of minerals, but good mineral specimens are not common. Crystals grow unobstructed only in cavities, joints and fissures. Just a few minerals make up most of the volume of rocks in the Earth's crust. These are called *rock-forming minerals*, most of which are silicates. The main ones are quartz, alkali and plagioclase feldspars, muscovite and biotite micas, pyroxenes (especially augite), amphiboles (especially hornblende) and olivine. Calcite (calcium carbonate) is an important rock-forming mineral in sedimentary rocks, as is dolomite.

Mineral deposits are unusual concentrations of minerals that have formed by special processes, and may be present at sufficiently high levels to warrant extracting. There are several ways in which these are formed.

When magma cools to form igneous rocks, minerals may become concentrated in particular areas. Economic deposits of native elements, such as platinum, have been found in this setting, as have some oxides, such as magnetite, and sulphides such as pyrite and chalcopyrite.

Pegmatites often contain large crystals of minerals that would normally occur only in minute amounts. Pegmatites are formed during the last stages of crystallization of the magma, when the liquid is rich in water and many uncommon elements. Pegmatites commonly form veins and dykes around or within granite masses. Economic deposits of quartz, feldspar and mica form in this way. Pegmatites also yield

Introduction

such gemstones as beryl, garnet, topaz and tourmaline.

During the late stages of cooling of a magma, heated gases containing volatile elements such as boron, chlorine and fluorine stream out into the adjacent country rock. Minerals containing these elements will eventually crystallize as *pneumatolitic ore deposits*. These are common around granite intrusions, and may include tourmaline, topaz and fluorite.

During the final stages of cooling, hot fluids called *hydrothermal solutions* may react with the host rock to form replacement deposits, or precipitate into cracks and fissures to form veins. These may contain economically important minerals known as *ore*, together with minerals of no commercial value, known as *gangue*.

When mineral veins are exposed to weathering, they may be drastically altered. Secondary deposits are formed by the reaction of minerals at the surface with air and water. Solutions that leach down from the vein may react with primary ores, forming a zone of oxidized ores above the water table, and a zone of *secondary (supergene) sulphide enrichment* below it.

Sometimes the host rock may react with hot fluids to produce new minerals, a process called *metasomatism*. The term *skarn* is used for limestones that have been altered to form a variety of minerals, including epidote, olivine, vesuvianite, and ugrandite garnets, together with some ore minerals and boron-bearing minerals such as tourmaline.

The weathering of sedimentary rocks by wind and water may alter their composition, removing some components and concentrating others. These deposits may contain original minerals that are less prone to weathering, such as tin, gold, baryte and kyanite, or entirely new ones. An example of the latter type is bauxite, an important ore of aluminium.

Detrital deposits are sediments formed by the breakdown of existing rocks. In *placer deposits*, minerals that existed in only small amounts in the parent rock may become concentrated. In *alluvial deposits* (carried by a river), minerals are separated out according to density, and chemically resistant minerals, such as gold, cassiterite, ruby and garnet, may form important deposits.

Mineral deposits are also precipitated due to the evaporation of sea water. Halite and anhydrite are formed in this way. Evaporites can also form in desert areas, such as where transitory lakes dry out.

GEMSTONES

Gemstones have long been prized for their beautiful colours, attractive lustres and crystal forms. These minerals were thought to have special properties, some of which brought luck to the wearer, while others were thought to be capable of warding off or curing diseases. The mineral nephrite (a variety of jade) is named from the Greek *nephros*, meaning 'kidney', due to its alleged powers in protecting the wearer against kidney complaints. Findings in prehistoric caves in Europe have shown that gold and amber have been used for jewellery for several thousand years. Serpentine and obsidian have probably been used for much longer.

The beauty of a mineral may depend on its colour, transparency or lustre. Red rubies and green emeralds are attractively coloured, transparent and brilliant, whereas diamonds owe their popularity to their lustre and fire (the way they disperse light). The beauty of turquoise is in its azure-blue colour.

Rarity is an important factor in determining the value of a gem, as is durability. A gem should be able to resist physical and chemical damage. Softer gemstones, such as opal and peridot (olivine), are likely to lose their brilliance and colour in time and are unsuitable for setting in rings.

Many gemstones have become famous in their own right. For example, the largest diamond ever found was the Cullinan. This diamond measures about 12.5 cm (5 in) across, and was found at Premier Mine (South Africa) in 1905. It weighed 3106 metric carats (more than 1.3 lbs). It was cut into 105 gemstones, the largest of which weighs 516 carats and is known as the Star of Africa. It is set in the British Royal Sceptre.

Other famous diamonds include the Indian *Koh-i-noor* (Persian for 'Mountain of Light'), which was presented to Queen Victoria in 1850. The history of this diamond has been traced back to 1304. It has changed hands several times as a result of war and conquest.

Transparent varieties of beryl are popular as gemstones. The photograph shows green emerald, pale blue aquamarine, yellow heliodor, pink morganite and colourless goshenite. To show off their best qualities the gems are cut and polished, the many facets reflecting light back out of the crystal. The pale heliodor at the left shows the oblong emerald cut typically used for beryl.

Introduction

ROCKS

With few exceptions, geologists classify rocks in three groups according to the way they were formed. These groups are *igneous*, *metamorphic* or *sedimentary* rocks.

IGNEOUS ROCKS

Igneous rocks, such as basalts and granites, are those produced from hot magma rising up from the lower crust or upper mantle, which then cools and solidifies. *Extrusive* igneous rocks form from magma that is ejected from the crust (as in volcanoes) and cools on the surface, while *intrusive* rocks form from magma solidifying underground. Intrusive rocks may eventually be exposed at the surface, however, if the rock above them is weathered away.

Two main factors affect the nature of igneous rocks – the cooling rate of the magma and its chemical constitution. When magma reaches the Earth's surface as lava and flows either onto land or into the oceans, or is violently ejected, cooling is very rapid. This results either in *fine-grained* rocks, such as basalt, which are made up of tiny crystals, or *glassy* rocks, such as obsidian, where there has not been enough time for crystals to grow. On the other hand, when magmas are emplaced in the Earth's crust as *igneous intrusions*, they cool slowly and crystals have more time to grow. In very large intrusions, cooling is extremely slow, and *coarse-grained* rocks are formed, such as granites and gabbros. Smaller intrusions are characterized by *medium-grained* rocks, such as dolerite.

Plutons are large intrusions, often of granite, that extend deep down into the crust. Intrusions called *batholiths* cover up to hundreds of thousands of square kilometres in area. Smaller bodies (up to tens of square kilometres) are called *stocks*. *Dykes* and *sills* are sheet-like bodies of igneous rock which vary in size from centimetres to hundreds of metres wide. Dykes are vertical or near-vertical, cutting across bedding planes of sedimentary rocks, while sills usually follow them and are essentially horizontal. *Veins* are small irregular networks.

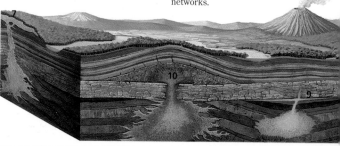

Volcanic rocks also occur in different forms. Basic lavas are of low viscosity and can flow from fissures over large areas. These are called *plateau lavas*. Rapid cooling under water gives rise to *pillow lavas* named after their characteristic shape. When lava and fragments (*pyroclasts*) are ejected from pipe-like vents, they form volcanic cones.

The formation of the oceanic crust is a mixture of extrusive and intrusive processes. This particular type of igneous rock is important, because vast quantities are produced at the ocean ridges. *Ophiolites* are exposed pieces of oceanic crust that are pushed above sea level.

Texture

The most important textural feature of an igneous rock is its grain size. The crystals in fine-grained rocks cannot be distinguished with the naked eye, because they measure less than 0.1mm (0.004in) across. Medium-grained rocks contain crystals that may be distinguished by eye, between about 0.1mm and 2mm (0.004–0.08in), while coarse-grained rocks have grains that are larger than 2mm (0.08in).

Often the magma is not completely molten, but contains crystals of minerals that have a high melting point. On cooling, these large crystals are surrounded by finer-grained material known as the *matrix*. They are especially

This section through a volcanic region shows the formation of igneous rocks. Magma rises from a large underground chamber **1**, up the volcano's central vent **2** or through a side vent **3**. During eruptions, ash **4**, which consists of tiny fragments of magma, may be shot into the air and lava **5** flows out of the vent. Many volcanoes are composed of alternating layers of ash and lava **6**. Lava can also reach the surface through fissures **7** where it spreads out without building a volcano. Magma which hardens on the surface forms extrusive igneous rocks. Some magma hardens underground to create intrusive igneous rocks. Steeply inclined sheets of magma form dykes **8**. Sills **9** are parallel to existing beds. Bodies called loccoliths **10** push up the overlying rocks into domes. The largest masses of magma are batholiths (not shown here). Steep-sided volcanoes such as this, which produce a lot of ash, are formed from acid to intermediate magma. Most dykes and sills, however, are produced by the more fluid basic lavas.

noticeable in the finer-grained rocks. Such *phenocrysts* may be included in the name of the rock, as in olivine basalt.

Structure

The structure of a rock refers to features that are on a larger scale than the textural relationship between the component grains:

Layered or **banded structure** is made apparent by differently coloured or textured bands.

Vesicular structure is caused when bubbles of gas escape from a magma leaving cavities (*vesicles*) in the rock. If these vesicles are filled with secondary minerals they are called *amygdales*.

Xenoliths are pieces of other rock embedded in an igneous rock. They are usually fragments of host rock which fall into the magma.

amygdaloidal structure

vesicular structure

Colour

Rocks containing mainly light-coloured or *felsic* minerals are termed *leucocratic*. With increasing content of dark-coloured or *mafic* minerals, the rock becomes *melanocratic*. If dark minerals make up more than 90 per cent, the rock is called *ultramafic*. Most coloured minerals are

magnesium- and iron-bearing (*ferromagnesian*), and include olivines and pyroxenes. The colour comes from the iron. The *colour index* is the percentage of dark-coloured minerals in a rock. It is usually estimated and can be seen only in coarse- to medium-grained rocks.

Mineralogy

The minerals encountered most frequently in igneous rocks act as a means of classification. Referred to as *essential minerals*, they come from a relatively small group of rock-forming silicates. These are the light-coloured minerals quartz, the feldspars and feldspathoids and the dark-coloured pyroxenes, olivines, micas and amphiboles. Most rocks contain relatively few, perhaps two to four, essential minerals. Minerals occurring in minor amounts in the rock are called *accessory minerals*. Rocks with a colour index of less than 90 per cent are classified using the QAPF diagram shown on page 25. The diagram consists of two triangles, QAP and APF, where Q=quartz, A=alkali feldspar, P=plagioclase and F=feldspathoid. A rock can be plotted on the diagram, and named, according to the relative proportions of its felsic minerals.

Rocks are also classified chemically by the quantity of silica (SiO_2) they contain. This may be chemically combined, as in the silicate minerals, or if sufficient silica is present it forms free quartz. The rock is then said to be *oversaturated*. Rocks may be classed as *acid*, *intermediate*, *basic* or *ultrabasic*, as the content of silica decreases.

1 Quartzolite and quartz-
   rich granitoids
2 Alkali feldspar granite
3 Granite
4 Granodiorite
5 Tonalite
6 Alkali feldspar syenite
7 Syenite
8 Monzonite
9 Monzodiorite
   and monzogabbro
10 Diorite, gabbro and
   anorthosite
11 Feldspathoid syenite
12 Feldspathoid
   monzosyenite
13 Feldspathoid
   monzodiorite and
   feldspathoid
   monzogabbro
14 Feldspathoid diorite and
   feldspathoid gabbro
15 Foidolite

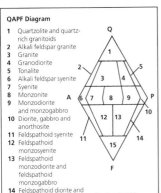

Q + A + P = 100
A + P + F = 100

The QAPT diagram is used to classify igneous rocks.
The different regions represent rocks of different
composition. A rock in which the felsic minerals were
100 per cent quartz would plot at point Q and would
therefore be called a quartzolite.

METAMORPHIC ROCKS

Metamorphic rocks are produced by the alteration of all types of rocks in the solid state under high temperatures and/or pressures. This involves changes in mineralogy (recrystallization of existing minerals or formation of new ones) and usually changes in texture compared with the original rock type. The major group of metamorphic rocks have undergone *regional metamorphism*, usually during mountain-forming episodes, when the rocks are subjected to elevated pressures and temperatures. The forces involved in building mountain chains, such as the Alps and Himalayas, cause the rocks to be broken to form *faults* and bent to form *folds*. Areas of several hundred kilometres may be

The diagram below shows how pressure and heat during mountain building metamorphoses the sedimentary rock shale into slate. Heat from magma transforms limestones into the metamorphic rock marble.

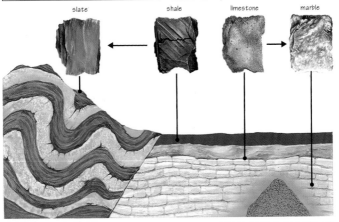

slate   shale   limestone   marble

Introduction

affected. *Dynamic metamorphism* refers to the alteration of rocks under higher pressures but lower temperatures. *Contact*, or *thermal metamorphism* occurs around igneous intrusions where the heat of the intrusion 'bakes' the surrounding country rock to form a *contact metamorphic aureole*. The size of such aureoles depends on such factors as the volume and temperature of the intruded magma. The degree of metamorphism is referred to as the *grade*. It increases from low- to medium- to high-grade with increasing temperatures and pressures. Higher grade rocks have a texture (or fabric) that is more crystalline and less like the original rock, and contain certain minerals (*index minerals*) which form only above specific temperature and pressure conditions.

Texture

Texture is an important aid to identification. Metamorphic rocks vary in grain size, becoming coarser with increasing temperature. Thus *slates* are fine-grained, *schists*, medium-grained and *gneisses* are coarse-grained. If the grains are roughly the same size, the texture is described as *granoblastic*. However, some minerals grow better than others and may form large, well-shaped crystals surrounded by a finer-grained matrix, giving rise to a *porphyroblastic* texture. If these crystals contain inclusions of smaller ones they are called *poikiloblasts*.

The recrystallization of minerals under pressure often causes the grains in the rock to be arranged in layers, known as *foliation*. Slates are characterized by a closely-spaced foliation, whereas *schistose* rocks have roughly parallel layers. Gneisses show a layered structure (*gneissose foliation*), with bands of quartz and feldspar alternating with bands of darker minerals. Hornfels is a hard rock produced by contact metamorphism, that usually has no directional alignment of crystals.

Structure

Original sedimentary and igneous structures (or *relict* structures) may be preserved. *Bedding* (layering) is the most obvious sedimentary structure. Features such as fossils and graded bedding, which can be used to find the original top of the bed, may also be preserved. Such structures are better preserved in low-grade rocks.

The main metamorphic features are *cleavage* and *folding*. Cleavage allows such rocks as slates and phyllites to split into sheets along parallel planes of foliation developed during metamorphism. There is no relationship between the original bedding and the imposed cleavage, so *cleavage planes* are usually at an angle to bedding. Most regionally metamorphosed rocks are folded to some degree. Folds vary in size from millimetre to kilometre scale.

schistosity

folding

Colour

Metamorphic rocks are commonly light to dark grey, but there are several exceptions with a distinctive colour that is useful in identification. Quartzite and pure marble can be recognized by their sparkling white colour, and mica shists are characterized by shiny flakes of silver or black mica. Glaucophane schists are slate blue, while eclogites are a striking red and green. Serpentinites are also distinctive, with red and green streaks or blotches and a waxy appearance.

Mineralogy

The total number of minerals appearing in a metamorphic rock is called the *assemblage* and is usually relatively few, especially if the rock had *equilibrated*, that is, recrystallization was completed. The type of minerals that appear in a particular grade of metamorphic rock depends on the composition of the original rock.

SEDIMENTARY ROCKS

Sediments which form rocks originate through physical or chemical processes, or through the accumulation of organic remains. The sediments may then be buried, compacted and converted into rocks, a process known as *lithification*. The most common sedimentary rock type is formed from *detrital* or *clastic sediments*. These are produced where existing rocks are weathered and eroded, mainly by the mechanical actions of rain, rivers, wind and glaciers, together with the chemical action of water and dissolved materials. Water, wind or moving ice then transport the fragments and deposit them as *sediments*. Water-borne material is deposited in rivers, in lakes or the sea. These sediments accumulate up to several kilometres thick. On burial they are compacted by

Around these hot springs in Turkey, the mineral-rich water precipitates calcite, as travertine. This has created a series of terraces.

Introduction

overlying material and may be cemented by percolating waters to form a rock.

The second most common sedimentary rock type is formed by the accumulation of organic matter from plants or animals. The most abundant organic sediment is derived from the calcium carbonate skeletons of marine animals such as shells and corals, forming limestones. Coal and oil are economically important sediments formed from organic matter.

The third type of sedimentary rocks are *evaporites*, formed by the precipitation of salts in hot dry regions from shallow seas and lakes.

Texture

The main textural feature of detrital rocks is the grain size, which refers to particles making up the sediment. They vary enormously, from boulders to microscopic clay particles. Grain size is classified by the following grades: *coarse* – more than 2mm (0.08in) in gravels; *medium* – 0.0625 to 2mm (0.02–0.08in) in sands; *fine* – 0.0039 to 0.0625mm (0.0015–0.02in) in silt; and less than 0.0039mm (0.0015in) in clay. Fine-grained rocks are called *argillaceous*, medium-grained, *arenaceous* and coarse-

grained, *rudaceous*. Extensive transport of detrital grains by water produces rounded grains, and continued reworking by currents as in beach areas sorts them into roughly the same size. Thus a sediment with rounded, well-sorted grains is called *mature*, while one with angular grains that range widely in size is called *immature*. The latter is unlikely to have been transported far from its source area. Wind-blown grains are often polished and almost spherical.

Structure

Sedimentary structures are usually very apparent in such rocks and are useful in understanding the environment in which deposition occurred.

Bedding is layering in the rock which can be picked out by varying textures, colours and mineralogies. It reflects episodes of rapid deposition followed by relatively little. Beds can vary in thickness. Those ranging in thickness from several metres down to centimetre size are called *strata*. Those less than a centimetre thick are called *laminations*. The surface

rudaceous texture

arenaceous texture

argillaceous texture

between layers is called the *bedding plane*. Although beds may be deposited horizontally, they are often tilted or folded by later Earth movements. Faulting is easily seen as the displacement of bedding planes.

Current bedding forms overlapping wedges. It is caused by deposition, often of sand, on a surface sloping in the direction of the current. The current may be of wind or water, and such bedding may range from a centimetre thick if formed in weak water currents, up to the size of a sand dune.

graded bedding

bedding

fine grains

↓

coarse grains

Graded bedding displays a variation of grain size within a bed from coarse at the bottom to fine at the top. This occurs when a mass of sediment has been deposited quickly, without sorting, so that the larger grains fall most rapidly, as in greywackes. Graded bedding indicates which way up the beds were formed in highly folded rocks.

Ripple marks are the lines of ridges formed by water or wind movement preserved on the bedding plane at the top of a stratum.

Unconformities reflect the gaps in the sedimentary record between periods of deposition. They sometimes represent hundreds of millions of years during which the underlying rocks were often faulted and/or folded, then eroded. When new beds are deposited on these older strata, the surface between them is apparent as an unconformity. If the time interval was short, the underlying rocks may have remained horizontal and so the unconformity may not be obvious in the field.

Colour

The colour of a sedimentary rock is of limited use in identification. Pure limestones are usually white or near to white. But most sediments are coloured to varying degrees by iron oxides (red) or by organic material (grey to black).

Mineralogy

The identification of minerals in sedimentary rocks is less important for classification than in igneous or metamorphic rocks. Most important is to recognize calcite in order to identify limestones, and to distinguish silica from feldspars when identifying sandstones.

Introduction

COLLECTING ROCKS AND MINERALS

Collecting rocks and minerals is a fascinating and rewarding hobby, and can be done either on your own or with others. Local libraries often have information about a local geological society where enthusiasts meet.

Equipment

To study rocks and minerals, some basic equipment is required. First, you will need a good hand lens, with a magnification of about x 10, and a geological hammer for field work. This should have a square head and a pick or chisel edge. A chisel may be useful for splitting open rocks. Always wear safety goggles when hammering, to protect your eyes from splinters of rock. It is advisable to wear a hard hat in certain areas and is essential if visiting a quarry. Sensible clothes are needed, including walking boots or shoes, and a small rucksack to transport your finds.

Each specimen should be numbered instantly using a felt tip pen, either directly, or on a label stuck on the specimen. The number should be entered into a notebook, together with notes on the locality, the date, and so on. Wrap specimens in newspaper to avoid chipping.

Where to start looking

A local museum is a good place to start, because it often contains representative samples of local materials. Once you decide to go on a collecting expedition, study a local geological map. This will not only guide you to interesting rocks but may also help you to avoid major misidentifications, which newcomers to the field can make all too easily. Also, study the topography so that you can set out suitably clothed. Make sure someone knows where you are going, especially in rugged terrain.

Good places to start are road cuttings, cliffs, quarries or stream beds. Take care to ask permission before venturing onto private land. When possible, collect from mine dumps, or from rock fallen from cliffs rather than indiscriminately hammering at fresh faces. Quite often the best specimens are found in this way.

Looking after your collection

Insoluble specimens may be cleaned with water and a little detergent, using a soft brush. Each specimen should be given a permanent number, written onto the specimen in Indian ink, or onto a spot of white acrylic paint. The specimen details and number should then be entered into a catalogue. It is then ready for display or storage. If you have difficulty in identifying a specimen, your local museum will be happy to help.

A word of caution

Enthusiastic but inexperienced collectors almost always return from an expedition overladen with samples that are subsequently discarded as duplicates. Collect only what you really need. Do not leave sharp fragments of rock lying about that might damage vehicle tyres or livestock. Some sites have now become so overworked that hammering is no longer permitted.

Acid (of igneous rocks) containing at least 10% quartz, and chemically composed of more than 65% silica.

Aeolian wind-blown.

Alkaline (of igneous rock) with a high content of alkali metals, namely sodium and potassium.

Amygdales vesicles found in volcanic rocks, originally formed by gas bubbles in the magma and later filled with secondary minerals.

An percentage of anorthite in plagioclase feldspar.

Arenaceous (of sedimentary rocks) with sand-sized grains (see p.28).

Argillaceous (of sedimentary rocks) fine-grained (see p.28).

Aureole country rock affected by contact metamorphism around an igneous intrusion (see p.26).

Basic (of igneous rocks) containing 45-55% silica.

Batholith large intrusion, often with no visible floor, up to 1000 km^2 (386 sq mi) in area.

Bioherm mound of organic remains in a reef, also called a reef knoll.

Biostrome laterally extensive reefs made up of shells.

Cementation deposition of cement (usually silica, calcite or iron hydrates) between the particles in a loose sediment, thus converting it to hard rock.

Clay minerals fine-grained, hydrous silicates formed by extensive weathering of other silicate minerals.

Columnar joints vertical joints common in basalts producing regular, hexagonal pillars of rock.

Concretion irregular or rounded mass formed by the precipitation of a new mineral within a sedimentary rock. Rounded forms are called nodules.

Craton area of the continental crust that has not been significantly deformed typically since Cambrian times. Cratons contain extensive crystalline basement rocks called shields.

Cross-stratification phenomenon occurring in ripples, sand waves and dunes where individual strata are laid down at an angle to the main bedding planes. Also known as cross, current, or false bedding.

Detrital (of sedimentary rocks) formed by the accumulation of rock fragments. Also called clastic (see p.28).

Diatom single-celled plant found in oceans and lakes with a skeleton composed of silica.

Druse irregularly shaped cavity containing minerals that project inwards from the cavity walls.

Dune bedding large-scale cross stratification formed by the movement of sand dunes. Usually several metres high.

Dyke vertical or near-vertical igneous intrusion that cuts across existing bedding or foliation in the host rock (see p.23).

Essential minerals minerals which define a rock and must be present in order to give it a particular name (see p.24).

Facies group of metamorphic rocks formed under a particular set of physical conditions from any rock type. Rocks of the greenschist, amphibolite and granulite facies are all formed at moderate pressures (depths of 10–30km), but at low, medium and high temperatures respectively.

Fault break in the rocks resulting in displacement either side.

Feldspathoids aluminosilicate minerals, similar to the feldspars but containing less silica.

Glossary

Felsic (of rocks) essentially composed of the light-coloured minerals feldspar and either feldspathoid or silica.

Ferromagnesian dark coloured iron- and/or magnesium-bearing minerals, including augite, biotite, hornblende and olivine (see p.24).

Flow texture alignment of needle-like or tabular crystals, formed when crystallization occurs while the molten rock is still flowing.

Fumarole small volcanic vent issuing gases but no lava.

Graded bedding with coarse grains at the bottom of the bed, grading to finer particles at the top (see p.29).

Granitoid group of plutonic igneous rocks containing quartz. Includes granodiorite and tonalite.

Granular texture comprising minerals of roughly equal size.

Graphic texture intergrowth of minerals, especially quartz and feldspar, resembling runic inscriptions.

Hydrothermal deposit minerals which crystallize from hot watery fluids in the late stages of formation of igneous rocks.

Intermediate (of igneous rocks) with a silica content of 52–65%, including syenite, trachyte, diorite and andesite.

Joints cracks and fissures in rocks with no displacement either side.

Lamination fine layering in sediments, only millimetres thick. Often forms the internal structure in beds.

Lithic pertaining to rocks.

Lithification alteration of loose sediments into a rock (see p.27).

Mafic (of rocks) essentially composed of dark-coloured minerals.

Marine transgression rise in sea level, causing submersion of a land mass and the deposition of marine sediment. Conversely, marine regression causes deposition to cease and erosion to commence.

Marl mudrock composed of roughly equal amounts of clay and calcite.

Matrix fine-grained material surrounding coarser grains. Also known as groundmass.

Metabasite metamorphosed basic rock.

Metapelite metamorphosed pelitic rock.

Metasediment metamorphosed sedimentary rock.

Metasomatism process which alters the composition of a mineral or rock by the addition or subtraction of chemical elements by the action of hot fluids (see p.20).

Ophiolite suite of rocks comprising pillow lavas, dykes, gabbros and ultrabasic rocks, thought to have formed from oceanic crust and now exposed at the surface (see p.23).

Ophitic (of igneous rocks) special type of poikilitic texture in which plagioclase is enclosed by pyroxene.

Orbicular texture concentric shells of a different texture and/or mineralogy from the parent rock.

Orogenic belt belt of rocks commonly characterized by deformation and folding, formed in a mountain-building episode.

Pelagic of the deep sea. Usually clays or oozes composed of tiny silica or calcium carbonate skeletons.

Pelitic (of rocks) characterized by a high aluminium and low calcium ontent, especially clays and shales.

Perlitic (of glassy rocks) containing irregular, spheroidal cracks which are formed by contraction during cooling.

Phenocrysts large igneous crystals which contrast markedly in size with the surrounding crystals (see p.23).

Phytoplankton small floating plants such as diatoms.

Plug roughly vertical and cylindrical

volcanic intrusion.

Pluton large, coarse-grained igneous intrusion (see p.22).

Pneumatolysis reaction of the hot gases given off by a cooling magma with the surrounding country rock (see p.20).

Poikilitic (of igneous rocks) where large crystals of the host rock enclose small, randomly oriented crystals of a different mineral.

Poikiloblastic (of metamorphic rocks) where a large crystal contains small inclusions of another mineral (see p.26).

Porphyritic (of igneous rocks) comprising large crystals (phenocrysts) set in a finer-grained or glassy groundmass.

Porphyroblast large, well-developed crystal that has grown in a metamorphic rock (see p.26).

Pyroclast fragment of volcanic rock scattered by explosive eruption.

Radiolaria single-celled marine animals with a skeleton of silica.

Relict structure structure of the original rock which has persisted through metamorphism (see p.26).

Ripple marks small-scale undulations found in the bedding planes of sandstones and siltstones (see p.29).

Rudaceous (of sedimentary rocks) refers to the coarsest clastic sediments, specifically gravels, conglomerates and breccias (see p.28).

Shields areas of crystalline basement rock associated with cratons.

Sill essentially horizontal, sheet-like igneous intrusion usually between two sedimentary beds, may be hundreds of metres thick.

Slump bedding produced when an overlying bed slumps down into a weak underlying bed.

Solid solution series of minerals where there is complete gradation in composition between end members.

Spherulites spherical or sub-spherical bodies with a radial arrangement of acicular crystals, often of feldspar.

Spilite fine-grained, basic igneous rocks richer in sodium and water than basalt, and containing albite rather than plagioclase.

Stock small batholith, with an area of less than 10 km^2 (see p.23).

Subhedral grains showing some crystal faces.

Sublimation process whereby a solid turns directly into a vapour on heating, without passing through a liquid phase.

Subophitic (of igneous rocks) with feldspar crystals partly enclosed by pyroxene crystals of the same size.

Succession series of sedimentary rocks deposited in sequence.

Suite group of rocks that are related to each other by a common origin or process.

Tectonism large-scale movements and deformation of the Earth's crust.

Ultrabasic (of igneous rocks) containing less than 45% silica.

Ultramafic (of igneous rocks) containing more than 90% dark minerals.

Unconformity surface between sedimentary strata representing a time gap between periods of deposition.

Vacuoles spaces left by materials in a magma that are easily vaporized, such as water and carbon dioxide.

Vein irregular network of foreign minerals deposited in a rock.

Xenolith piece of rock that is different in origin to the igneous rock surrounding it (see p.24).

Zooplankton small floating animals such as radiolarians.

Gold *Au*

Gold nugget

Gold in quartz

Gold nugget

Gold has long been prized. Its value lies in its characteristic yellow colour, its rarity and its ability to be worked. It also has a high degree of resistance to chemical reactions, a property which makes it one of the so-called 'noble' metals. It does not dissolve in acids, apart from *aqua regia*. The old symbol for gold was a circle, a reflection of its ancient identity with the Sun. Gold is used in jewellery and was used in coinage. It has uses in plating, scientific instruments, medicine and dentistry. The largest gold nugget recorded was 214 kg (472 lb). It was found in 1872 at Holterman's Reef, New South Wales, Australia. The world's leading gold producers are South Africa and the Soviet Union. Many people mistake pyrite (fool's gold) and chalcopyrite for gold, but these minerals are harder and more brittle than gold.

GOLD

*Colour	characteristic yellow
*Lustre	metallic
Transparency	opaque; transmits greenish light in the thinnest sheets
Streak	yellow, lighter when alloyed with silver
*Hardness	2.5–3
Cleavage	none
Fracture	hackly; malleable
Habit	usually dendritic (branching) growths or disseminated grains; occasionally rounded nuggets and rarely octahedral, dodecahedral or cubic crystals
Twinning	common on octahedron
Specific gravity	19.3
Other tests	insoluble in single acids
Crystal system	cubic
*Alteration	none
Occurrence	in hydrothermal veins often associated with quartz; in alluvial deposits, notably stream or river sediments – separated from other minerals by its greater density; alluvial deposits may consolidate into rock
Examples	Witwatersrand (South Africa), Yukon (Canada), Porcupine (Canada), the Mother Lode, California, (USA) and the former USSR; very little in Europe, although used to be mined near Monte Rosa (Italy)

Silver on calcite

Wiry form

Silver

SILVER

*Colour	silver-white
Lustre	metallic
Transparency	opaque; very high reflectivity (95 per cent)
Streak	silver-white
Hardness	2.5–3
Cleavage	none
Fracture	hackly; malleable
Habit	commonly in a wiry form or as scales; crystals very rare
Twinning	common
Specific gravity	10.5
Other tests	dissolves in nitric acid and then precipitates white silver chloride on addition of common salt or hydrochloric acid; very good conductor of electricity and heat
Crystal system	cubic
*Alteration	tarnishes to black sulphide
Occurrence	in the oxidized zone of hydrothermal sulphide veins, and as primary ore in such veins
Examples	best known primary silver deposit is at Kongsberg (Norway); other well-known deposits include the Comstock Lode, Nevada (USA), Freiberg (Germany) and San Luis Potosí (Mexico)

Silver is a metal that is prized for much the same reasons as gold, although it is somewhat more chemically reactive. It is widely distributed but in small amounts, being rarer than gold. Throughout history, craftsmen have made silver jewellery – silver beads found in Egypt date back around 6000 years. Silver was also used for coins before copper-nickel alloy came into use. Silver is the best known reflector of light, which makes it useful in plating. Its extremely high electrical conductivity ensures a high demand in electronics. The instability of silver halides to light forms the basis of classical photographic techniques. The old symbol for silver was the Moon.

Copper *Cu*

Copper

malachite coating

Branching form

Copper with tarnish

tarnish

Massive form

COPPER

*Colour	light rose on fresh surface
Lustre	metallic
Transparency	opaque
Streak	metallic copper-red
*Hardness	2.5–3
Cleavage	none
Fracture	hackly; malleable, ductile
Habit	usually dendritic or wiry; rare crystals usually cubic or dodecahedral
Twinning	common
Specific gravity	8.95
Other tests	readily soluble in nitric acid
Crystal system	cubic
*Alteration	slight alteration gives characteristic copper-red colour; black copper oxide gives a dull brown colour; green carbonate on exposed surfaces
Occurrence	as hydrothermal and metasomatic deposits; it fills cracks and amygdales in basaltic lava flows as well as partially replacing other minerals therein especially those containing iron; also part of the cement in conglomerates and sandstones
Examples	best crystals found in the Keweenawan Peninsula (USA); others found in Italy, USA, Sweden, Chile, Germany, the former USSR and Zambia

Although it usually occurs in small quantities, native copper is widely distributed. This fact, together with its malleability and resistance to weathering, explains why it has long been used to make ornaments, tools and weapons. Bronze, an alloy of copper and tin which is much harder than pure copper, was first used in large quantities around 3000 BC. Brass, an alloy of copper and zinc, is a popular metal because of its attractive polished finish. Because copper is cheap, ductile (pliant) and a good conductor of electricity, it is widely used in the electrical industry. The name comes from the word for Cyprus, where copper has been mined since ancient times.

Platinum nugget

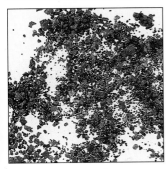

Platinum grains

Platinum is a rare and precious metal that occurs as a native element. It resembles silver, but it is less reactive and does not tarnish in air. Its greater hardness, higher density and high melting point – 1769°C (3216°F) against 962°C (1764°F) – also distinguish it from silver. These properties, together with its malleability and thermal stability make it useful for laboratory tongs and crucibles, electrical contacts in thermo couples, and for jewellry. Platinum is also an exceptionally good catalyst, used in the chemical and petroleum industries. Like gold, another noble metal, the only common acid combination to dissolve it is hot *aqua regia*, a mixture of concentrated hydrochloric and nitric acids. Native platinum contains lesser amounts of other related native elements, namely iridium, osmium, palladium and rhodium. The refining of platinum is the principle source of these other 'heavy metals'. Platinum derives its name from the Spanish *platina*, a diminutive form of *plata*, meaning 'silver'.

PLATINUM

Colour	grey-white to light grey
Lustre	metallic
Transparency	opaque
Streak	white, steel-grey
Hardness	4–4.5
Cleavage	absent
Fracture	hackly; ductile
Habit	rare cubic crystals; usually as grains, scales or nuggets
*Specific gravity	21.5 when pure; natural material usually 14–19, mainly due to dissolved iron and copper
Other tests	insoluble in single acids; occasionally magnetic
Crystal system	cubic
*Alteration	none
Occurrence	segregations, alongside chromite in ultrabasic igneous rocks, especially dunites; in norites with immiscible sulphide deposits; as placer deposits in stream or river sediments, separated by its high density; non-native platinum occurs in the mineral sperrylite (PtAs$_2$)
Examples	segregations in the Bushveld Complex (South Africa) and the Ural Mountains (the former USSR); sulphide deposits in Sudbury (Canada); placer deposits in the Urals (the former USSR), Colombia and the USA

Arsenic *As*

Mammilated form

Concentrically layered mass

Arsenic is a fairly rare mineral which is found in hydrothermal veins in association with silver-cobalt-nickel ores. In this form, it rarely occurs in sufficient quantity to make extraction viable. However, it occurs widely in combination, particularly in sulphide ores. Most commercial arsenic is obtained from other arsenic-bearing minerals such as arsenopyrite. The oxide As_2O_3 (white arsenic) is the most widely used form of arsenic. It is obtained from the flue-dust produced in the smelting of arsenic ores. From about 2000 BC, metal-workers have used about 4 per cent arsenic in copper goods to make them harder and stronger. Arsenic is still used in some special alloys. It is poisonous which makes it useful in pesticides, preservatives and, in the pharmaceutical industry, for treating parasitic illnesses. It derives its name from the Greek word *arsenikon* meaning 'masculine', because metals were believed to be different sexes. The term was first applied to the mineral orpiment because of its potent properties.

ARSENIC

Colour	light grey, tarnishing rapidly to dark grey
Lustre	metallic
Transparency	opaque
Streak	light grey
Hardness	3.5
Cleavage	basal, perfect
Fracture	uneven; brittle
Habit	crystals rare (artificial ones pseudo-cubic); generally granular, massive or concentrically layered botryoidal or stalactitic masses
Twinning	rare
Specific gravity	5.7
*Other tests	smells like garlic on heating or striking with a hammer
Crystal system	trigonal
Occurrence	in hydrothermal veins usually associated with ores of silver, cobalt and nickel, in igneous and metamorphic rocks
Examples	Gikos, Siberia (Russia), Erzgebirge and the Harz Moutains (Germany), Washington Camp, Santa Cruz County (USA), France, Italy, Romania, the former Czechoslovakia

Antimony

Massive form

ANTIMONY

Colour	light grey
Lustre	metallic
Transparency	opaque
Streak	grey
Hardness	3–3.5
Cleavage	basal, perfect; rhombohedral, good
Fracture	uneven; very brittle
Habit	crystals rare; usually massive and reniform (kidney-shaped); sometimes lamellar with a cleavage through the mass
Twinning	common, repeated
Specific gravity	6.6–6.7
Crystal system	trigonal
Occurrence	in hydrothermal veins often accompanying silver or arsenic; associated minerals are stibnite, sphalerite, galena and pyrite
Examples	Sala (Sweden), Andreasberg (Germany), Coimbra (Portugal), Val Cavargna and Sardinia (Italy), New Brunswick (Canada), Kern County, California (USA), Saranoak (Borneo)

Native antimony is found only in small quantities in hydrothermal veins, where it is formed by reactions of antimony–sulphur minerals. As antimony occurs rarely as a native element, the economic sources of this metal are ores, mainly stibnite (Sb_2S_3). Antimony is alloyed with lead to make type-metal and bullets, because it lowers the melting point and increases the hardness of the lead. Alloyed with copper and tin, it produces low-friction Babbitt metal, used for bearings. Antimony and its compounds are poisonous and are used in drugs for the treatment of parasitic diseases. The name comes from the Latin *antimonium*. The chemical symbol for antimony, Sb, comes from the Latin *stiborum*, meaning 'mark'. Black stibnite has been used at least since Ancient Egyptian times as mascara for painting eyebrows and eyelashes.

Bismuth *Bi*

oxide coating

Bismuth

Small globules on matrix

Native form

Bismuth is a semi-metal that occurs rarely as a native element. It is related to arsenic and antimony in structure and has similar physical properties. They are all brittle and are poorer conductors of heat and electricity than metals. Bismuth is not of great economic importance, most of that produced is used for medicines and cosmetics. It is also used with cadmium, lead or tin to make low-melting alloys, such as Wood's metal which melts at 70°C (158°F). Such alloys are useful in electrical fuses and fire protection devices. Like antimony, bismuth is also used for fine castings. Artificially produced crystals of bismuth can be attractive because of their good cleavage and form, together with their high lustre. Bismuth is produced mainly as a by-product from the smelting of sulphide ores.

BISMUTH

*Colour	silver-white, tarnishing to reddish tinge, sometimes iridescent
Lustre	metallic
Transparency	opaque
Streak	silver-white, shiny
Hardness	2–2.5
*Cleavage	basal, perfect
Fracture	uneven; sectile
Habit	crystals rare; massive, granular or in branching, net-like forms
Twinning	common, repeated
Specific gravity	9.7–9.8
*Other tests	melts readily at 271°C (520°F), giving an orange-yellow oxide coating; dissolves in nitric acid
Crystal system	trigonal
Occurrence	in hydrothermal veins, often associated with gold, silver, tin, nickel, cobalt and lead
Examples	Oruro and Tasna (Bolivia), Cornwall (England), Erzgebirge (Germany), Kongsberg (Norway), Ontario (Canada); small amounts at Monroe, Connecticut and in Summit and Boulder counties, Colorado (USA)

c Diamond

Cut and polished diamond

Diamond in kimberlite

Diamond is composed of pure carbon, like graphite. But the atoms in diamond have been forced into a compact three-dimensional structure by the high pressures in the upper mantle, where it is formed. Hence diamond is much harder and has a higher specific gravity than graphite. This is reflected in its name, which comes from the Greek word for 'invincible'. Gem-quality diamonds are colourless, transparent and unflawed. Low-quality diamonds are used as industrial abrasives. Varieties of diamond are *bort*, which has a rounded, fibrous, radiate structure, and *carbonado*, which is black and microcrystalline. Diamond is mined from kimberlite and alluvial deposits. The largest recorded diamond is the Cullinan, from the Transvaal in South Africa. Uncut it weighed 3106 carats (1 carat equals 0.2 g or 0.007 oz).

DIAMOND

Colour	colourless, but may be coloured by yellow, red, brown, grey or black impurities
*Lustre	brilliantly adamantine to greasy
Transparency	transparent, but can be translucent to opaque when very dark coloured and of poor crystallinity
Streak	white
*Hardness	10
*Cleavage	octahedral, perfect
Fracture	conchoidal
Habit	octahedral crystals often with curved faces, sometimes dodecahedral, rarely tetrahedral; frequently of flattened habit
Twinning	sometimes, on octahedron
Specific gravity	3.5
Crystal system	cubic
Occurrence	rare and in ultrabasic rocks of deep origin called kimberlites which form roughly cylindrical pipes or sometimes dykes, found in continental shield areas; also found in deposits in rivers running from such rocks
Examples	most important fields are those of Kimberley (South Africa); also in Tanzania, Yakutia (former USSR), India, Brazil and Namibia

41

Graphite *C*

Graphite

cleavage surfaces

Graphite

Graphite

Graphite, like diamond, is a form of pure carbon. The carbon atoms in graphite are joined together in hexagonal arrays in two-dimensional sheets stacked one on top of another. This gives graphite its characteristic basal cleavage and flaking, which imparts a greasy feel and gives it lubricant properties. Graphite is also known as plumbago or black lead. Its softness and black streak have long made it a writing tool, especially in pencils. It is also used in crucibles, electrodes, generator brushes, and as a moderator to slow down neutrons in atomic reactors. Its colour, streak and lower specific gravity distinguish it from molybdenite. Graphite is formed mainly when sediments rich in organic matter are metamorphosed.

GRAPHITE

Colour	black
Lustre	dull, metallic
Transparency	opaque
***Streak**	black, shiny
Hardness	1–2
***Cleavage**	basal, perfect
Habit	usually as scales and foliated or earthy masses or as compact lumps; occasionally as six-sided flat, tabular crystals
***Specific gravity**	2.1–2.2
***Other tests**	greasy feel; thin flakes broken off along cleavage are flexible; conducts electricity
Crystal system	hexagonal
Occurrence	mainly in metamorphosed sediments, usually marbles, schists and gneisses; also in metamorphosed coal; sometimes associated with basic igneous rocks, pegmatites and quartz veins possibly from volcanic gases; also in meteorites
Examples	production mainly in the former USSR, Mexico, Korea, Austria, Sri Lanka and Madagascar; in Europe, economic deposits in the former Czechoslovakia, Germany and Italy. Crystals in marble at Ogdensburg, New York and in gneiss at Edison, New Jersey (USA)

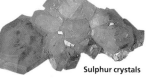

resinous lustre

Sulphur crystals

Massive sulphur

Sulphur crystals

SULPHUR

*Colour	yellow to yellow-brown
Lustre	resinous
Transparency	transparent to translucent
Streak	white
*Hardness	1.5–2.5
Cleavage	none
Fracture	uneven to conchoidal
Habit	bipyramids or thick tablets; also encrusting, stalactitic, massive or powdery
Specific gravity	2–2.1
*Other tests	low melting point, 113°C (235°F); burns with a bluish flame to give the toxic gas sulphur dioxide; soluble in carbon disulphide
Crystal system	orthorhombic
Occurrence	encrustations around volcanic vents and fumaroles caused by sublimation; precipitates in hot springs caused by reaction of the dissolved gases H_2S and SO_2; associated with gypsum and bituminous materials in Tertiary shales, sandstones and limestones; in the cap rock of salt domes
Examples	produced in Louisiana and Texas (USA) from salt domes; in Sicily from Tertiary sediments. Volcanic sulphur deposits in Japan, Indonesia and S American Andes

Sulphur is a soft, low-density mineral that has a bright yellow colour when pure. Although still obtained from natural deposits, much sulphur is now produced as a by-product in oil refining. Sulphur is used in the manufacture of sulphuric acid, gunpowder, insecticides and matches. It is also the vulcanizing (hardening) agent for rubber. Sulphur crystals belong to the orthorhombic crystal system, the finest examples coming from Sicily and the Romagna, Italy. Sulphur also occurs in two other crystal forms belonging to the monoclinic crystal system, b-sulphur and g-sulphur. Both of these are formed at higher temperatures. They rarely occur naturally. The name is thought to come from the Indo-European words meaning 'to burn slowly'.

Pyrite FeS_2

Pyrite nodule

Pyritohedron

striations

Cubic crystals in slate

Purite and quartz

Commonly known as 'fool's gold', pyrite is an abundant and widespread mineral. Its name comes from the Greek word for fire and refers to the sparks produced when pyrite is struck with a hammer. It is brass-yellow in colour, paler than gold and chalcopyrite, but slightly darker than marcasite. The ancient Greeks used pyrite for earrings and pins and the Incas may have used pyrite tablets as mirrors. It has been used since Victorian times in jewellery, though jewellers often call it marcasite. It was formerly used instead of flint in old wheel lock firearms. Pyrite is commonly mined for the copper and gold associated with it, but its chief use is as a source of sulphur, which is used in the manufacture of sulphuric acid and ferrous sulphate. This mineral is also known as pyrites or iron pyrites.

PYRITE

*Colour	bronze yellow to pale brass yellow; lacks tarnish
Lustre	metallic
Transparency	opaque
Streak	greenish or brownish black
Hardness	6–6.5
Cleavage	indistinct, cubic and octahedral
Fracture	conchoidal to uneven; brittle
Habit	as cubic crystals, often striated parallel to cube edges, also as octahedra and pyritohedra; massive, as granular aggregates or nodules with internally radiating structure
Twinning	frequent, looking like interpenetrating cubes, known as 'Iron Crosses'
Specific gravity	4.9–5.1
Other tests	emits sparks when struck; powder dissolves in nitric but not hydrochloric acid
Crystal system	cubic
Alteration	readily oxidizes to iron sulphate or the hydrated oxide limonite
Occurrence	in sedimentary rocks, especially black shales; often replaces fossils; an accessory mineral in igneous rocks; common in ore veins; in metamorphic rocks, especially slate
Examples	Spain, Italy, Norway, Cyprus, Tasmania and USA

Spear – shaped twinned crystal

Aggregate of crystals

Ancient writers used the term marcasite, which is of Arabic or Moorish origin, for bismuth and antimony. Later, mineralogists and miners used it as the name for pyrite and even today the so-called marcasite used for brooches and earrings is actually pyrite. Marcasite is very similar in appearance and of identical composition to pyrite. Its main distinguishing features are its paler colour (hence the alternative name 'white iron pyrites'), its lower specific gravity and its crystal system. 'Spearhead' forms of marcasite are characteristic. In the past, polished marcasite was used to make ornaments.

Aggregate of crystals

MARCASITE

*Colour	pale bronze-yellow to silvery on fresh surfaces
Lustre	metallic
Transparency	opaque
Streak	greyish or brownish black
Hardness	6–6.5
Cleavage	poor, prismatic
Fracture	uneven; brittle
Habit	as tabular crystals, often with curved faces; also massive, stalactitic or nodular, with internally radiating structure
*Twinning	commonly twinned to form 'cockscomb' aggregates and 'spearhead' forms
Specific gravity	4.8–4.9
Other tests	dissolves with difficulty in nitric acid, flakes of sulphur appearing in solution
Crystal system	orthorhombic
Alteration	decomposes to iron sulphate or limonite; may alter to pyrite; eventually crumbles to dust
Occurrence	formed under acid conditions, at lower temperatures than pyrite; in hydrothermal veins, often with lead and zinc ores; also as a precipitate in nodules in sedimentary rocks e.g. chalk; may replace fossils
Examples	England, Germany, the former Czechoslovakia, Romania and the USA

45

Arsenopyrite *FeAsS*

Crystals

Massive form

Arsenopyrite, also known as mispickel or arsenical pyrites, is the principal ore of arsenic and the most abundant arsenic mineral. Of widespread occurrence, its appearance is paler and more silvery than pyrite, with which it is commonly found. Its colour also distinguishes arsenopyrite from marcasite. It may tarnish, however, when exposed. It occurs in sulphide deposits associated with gold and cobalt, in a pegmatitic or pneumatolytic environment with tin and copper, and in high-temperature hydrothermal veins with gold, silver and nickel. Some varieties may contain traces of other metals. Cobalt, gold, silver and tin are by-products of the smelting process.

Crystals

ARSENOPYRITE

*Colour	silvery-white to steel-grey, tarnishing pale copper-colour on exposure
Lustre	metallic
Transparency	opaque
*Streak	black or dark grey
Hardness	5.5–6
Cleavage	good, parallel to dome faces
Fracture	uneven; brittle
Habit	forms elongated, striated prismatic crystals; may appear orthorhombic through twinning; also massive, as columnar aggregates; compact and granular
Twinning	cross-shaped twins common
Specific gravity	5.9–6.2
*Other tests	sparks when struck; soluble in nitric acid, giving sulphur; fuses easily, giving off a strong garlic smell
Crystal system	monoclinic
Occurrence	in sulphide deposits; also disseminated in limestones and dolomites; in pegmatites and hydrothermal veins; in small amounts in concretionary layers of siderite in black band ironstone
Examples	deposits occur in Norway, Sweden, Germany, the USA and Canada

Realgar is an orange-red mineral which can be distinguished from others of a similar colour by its streak. Realgar commonly occurs with lemon-yellow orpiment (As_2S_3), to which it readily alters. The term realgar comes from the Arabic *rahj al ghar* (meaning 'powder of the mine'), while the name orpiment is a corruption of the Latin *auripigmentum* (golden paint) – a reference not only to its colour, but also to the belief that it contained gold. Realgar is used in the manufacture of fireworks and paint. Orpiment is an ore of arsenic, occurring in arsenic veins, hot springs and volcanic deposits. It is used in tanning hides to remove hair.

Orpiment

Realgar crystals

Realgar with orpiment

orpiment

realgar

REALGAR

*Colour	orange to orange-red
*Lustre	resinous
Transparency	transparent to translucent
*Streak	orange to red
Hardness	1.5–2
Cleavage	good in one direction
Fracture	conchoidal or uneven; sectile
Habit	usually massive, in compact aggregates or as a scarlet incrustation; rarely as vertically striated, short prismatic crystals
Specific gravity	3.5–3.6
*Other tests	fuses easily, giving off arsenic fumes with a garlic smell; decomposed by nitric acid; association with orpiment
Crystal system	monoclinic
Alteration	decomposes on exposure to light and air to an orange-yellow powder of orpiment and arsenolite (AsS_2O_3)
Occurrence	in low-temperature ore veins associated with orpiment, stibnite or cinnabar; also in some limestones and clay rocks; occurs in volcanic lavas and as a hot spring deposit
Examples	Switzerland, Italy, Corsica, Romania and the USA

Chalcopyrite $CuFeS_2$

Massive form

Chalcopyrite

Chalcopyrite
with quartz

CHALCOPYRITE

*Colour	brass-yellow, often with a brown or iridescent tarnish
Lustre	metallic
Transparency	opaque
*Streak	greenish-black
*Hardness	3.5–4
Cleavage	poor
*Fracture	conchoidal to uneven; brittle
Habit	crystals uncommon, usually massive and compact
Twinning	frequent lamellar twinning
Specific gravity	4.1–4.3
Other tests	soluble in nitric acid; burns in flame, colouring it green and giving off toxic fumes
Crystal system	tetragonal
Alteration	to sulphates, malachite, azurite and limonite on exposure to moisture
Occurrence	in high- and medium-temperature veins with cassiterite, or galena and sphalerite, and as a 'porphyry copper' deposit in mafic volcanic rocks; in contact metamorphic rocks (skarns) and in placer deposits formed from the break-up of these rocks
Examples	Spain, France, Germany, Norway, Cyprus, Tasmania, the USA, Canada, Chile, the former USSR, Zaire and Zambia

Chalcopyrite or copper pyrites, is a brassy yellow, metallic mineral. It is one of the more common sulphides and the most common copper mineral. It can be distinguished from pyrite because it is usually deeper in colour, and, unlike pyrite, it crumbles when cut with a knife, and does not produce sparks when hit with a hammer. Unlike the similar pyrrhotite, it is non-magnetic. Its brittleness, streak and solubility in nitric acid distinguish it from gold. It is a major copper ore, producing four-fifths of the world's copper, and gold and silver as useful by-products. It occurs with bornite in sulphide deposits of the Copper Belt in Zambia, and also as grains in shale in the well-known Kupferschiefer of Mansfeld, Germany.

Massive form

fresh surface—

Bornite

Bornite, which is also known as Erubescite or Peacock ore, is characterized by its iridescent tarnish and the red colour of fresh surfaces. It will eventually turn black after prolonged exposure. It was called 'horse-flesh ore' in Cornwall, England, where it was once mined. Bornite is a common ore of copper, found in high-temperature veins, intrusive igneous rocks, pegmatites and contact metamorphic rocks. It is often associated with the minerals chalcopyrite and chalcocite. It was named after Ignatius von Born, a distinguished eighteenth-century mineralogist.

Massive form

Iridescent surface

BORNITE

*Colour	coppery red or bronze, rapidly tarnishes on exposure to become iridescent, with a purple and blue film
Lustre	metallic
Transparency	opaque
Streak	pale grey-black, slightly shining
*Hardness	3
Cleavage	poor
Fracture	subconchoidal or uneven; brittle
Habit	commonly as compact granular masses, or crystalline as cubes, dodecahedra or octahedra
Twinning	on octahedron
Specific gravity	4.9–5.4
Other tests	soluble in nitric acid, leaving a deposit of sulphur; fuses fairly easily, giving a magnetic globule
Crystal system	tetragonal (pseudo-cubic)
Alteration	alters to chalcocite, malachite, azurite
Occurrence	in pegmatites or hydrothermal veins; a common primary ore mineral of mixed sulphide veins; the dominant constituent of the copper deposits in the shales of the Kupferschiefer of Mansfeld (Germany)
Examples	England, Namibia, the USA and Tasmania

49

Chalcocite Cu_2S

Chalcocite in copper ore

Chalcocite crystals

Pseudohexagonal crystals

C halcocite (also called chalcosine or copper glance) is a valuable ore of copper. It commonly occurs in sulphide deposits where percolating water dissolves copper minerals near the surface and redeposits them below the water table. In this zone of secondary enrichment it is associated with bornite. In the weathered zone above, it is associated with azurite, cuprite and malachite. Chalcocite is an important 'porphyry copper' deposit. It also forms as a secondary deposit through the alteration of chalcopyrite. It forms attractive pseudo-hexagonal crystals in Cornwall, England, the Transvaal, South Africa and Bristol, Connecticut, USA. It is named after the Greek *chalkos*, meaning 'copper'.

CHALCOCITE

*Colour	black or lead-grey, often with greenish or bluish tarnish
Lustre	metallic
Transparency	opaque
Streak	black, may shine
Hardness	2.5–3
Cleavage	poor, parallel to prism faces
Fracture	conchoidal; brittle, sectile, almost malleable
Habit	usually massive with a compact or granular structure; rarely as prismatic crystals
Twinning	often gives stellate groups of three individuals
Specific gravity	5.5–5.8
Other tests	soluble in hot nitric acid, leaving a sulphur precipitate; colours a flame green, giving off fumes of sulphur dioxide
Crystal system	orthorhombic
Alteration	to malachite, azurite, covellite
Occurrence	in veins of hydrothermal sulphide deposits; may be associated with other copper minerals, e.g. cuprite, malachite, azurite
Examples	Cornwall (England), Kongsberg (Norway), Monte Catini (Italy), Tsumeb (Namibia), Butte, Montana (USA)

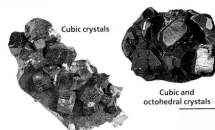

Cubic crystals

Cubic and octohedral crystals

brown surface alteration

Crystals

Crystals with gangue minerals

GALENA

*Colour	lead-grey, cleavage surfaces may blacken with time
*Lustre	metallic, tarnishing dull
Transparency	opaque
Streak	lead-grey
Hardness	2.5
*Cleavage	perfect cubic, breaking into smaller cubes when hit
Fracture	flat, even or conchoidal; brittle
*Habit	cubes, rarely octahedra; often massive, and coarsely or finely granular
Twinning	common, penetration or contact twins on octahedron
*Specific gravity	7.4–7.6
Other tests	soluble when heated in hydrochloric acid, giving off hydrogen sulphide with its characteristic smell of bad eggs; dissolves in nitric acid to produce small flakes of sulphur and a fine white precipitate
Crystal system	cubic
Occurrence	a hydrothermal mineral of medium-temperature deposits, often with sphalerite; also found in sedimentary rocks through the replacement of pre-existing rock by circulating waters
Examples	England, Australia, the USA, Mexico, Germany

G alena, the main ore of lead, is one of the most abundant and widely distributed sulphides. Because it almost always contains silver – up to 1 per cent – galena may also form an important source of silver. Galena is often found in hydrothermal veins, in association with chalcopyrite, pyrite and sphalerite, and also with the gangue minerals baryte, calcite, dolomite, fluorite and quartz. In higher temperature veins, associated minerals may be garnet, diopside and feldspar. Enormous deposits occur (with sphalerite) in the limestones and cherts of the Tri-State mining district of Missouri, Oklahoma and Kansas. The name is derived from the Greek for 'lead ore'. The most important use of lead is for making storage batteries, pipes and shot.

Cinnabar *HgS*

Adamantine crystals

Massive form

Tabular crystal

CINNABAR

*Colour	scarlet or red
Lustre	adamantine when crystalline
Transparency	transparent to translucent, or opaque when dull or earthy
*Streak	bright scarlet
Hardness	2–2.5
*Cleavage	perfect prismatic
Fracture	subconchoidal or uneven; somewhat sectile
Habit	rarely crystalline, as rhombohedra or as thick tabular crystals, also prismatic; earthy films, granular or massive
Twinning	common, basal
*Specific gravity	8–8.2
Other tests	insoluble in acids; mercury droplets form on wall when heated in a tube
Crystal system	trigonal
Occurrence	found in rocks, associated with volcanic activity, such as hot springs; also as low-temperature hydrothermal veins, and as replacement deposits in sedimentary rocks associated with igneous activity; may be found as alluvial deposits following erosion of older rocks
Examples	Spain, Yugoslavia, Italy, USA, the former USSR, China, and Mongolia

The poisonous mineral cinnabar is the most important ore of mercury, but is found in large quantities at few localities. The Chinese and others used it as the pigment vermilion. Native mercury, the only mineral which is liquid at room temperature, is occasionally found in cinnabar deposits. Mercury is used in the production of chemicals and paints and in thermometers and other instruments. The most important cinnabar deposits occur as masses and impregnations in lavas, cavernous limestones, and clays, in such places as Almadén, Spain, Idria, Yugoslavia and Monte Amiata, Italy. Minerals found in association with cinnabar are baryte, calcite, chalcedony, pyrite, quartz, realgar and stibnite. The name cinnabar is thought to have originated in India, where it is applied to a red resin.

Adamantine crystals

Tetrahedral crystal

The term sphalerite comes from the Greek *sphaleros*, meaning treacherous. This is because it has often been confused with galena, although it contains no lead. Similarly, it is also called zincblende or blende, from a German word meaning blind or deceiving. It is an important and common ore of zinc, often found with galena. By-products of sphalerite-working usually include cadmium, gallium and indium. Zinc is used as sheet zinc and for galvanizing iron. It is also a component of brass. Most sphalerite contains some iron, which affects its colour. Pure varieties are yellow or reddish-brown, but if the mineral contains more than 10 per cent iron, it appears black and is called *marmatite*.

Adamantine crystals

SPHALERITE

*Colour	commonly black or brown, sometimes yellow or white, rarely colourless
*Lustre	adamantine or resinous
Transparency	translucent or opaque
Streak	light yellow to brownish, or white
Hardness	3.5–4
*Cleavage	perfect, parallel to dodecahedron
Fracture	conchoidal; brittle
Habit	tetrahedra and dodecahedra common; also massive and compact, botryoidal or fibrous
Twinning	common on octahedron
Specific gravity	3.9–4.2
Other tests	pale varieties may fluoresce under ultraviolet light; soluble in hydrochloric acid, giving off hydrogen sulphide
Crystal system	cubic
Alteration	to limonite, hemimorphite or smithsonite
Occurrence	in hydrothermal vein deposits associated with galena, argentite, baryte, chalcopyrite and fluorite; in low- and high-temperature replacement deposits (skarns); in metamorphic rocks
Examples	Hungary, the former Yugoslavia, England, Spain, USA, Canada and Australia

Molybdenite MoS_2

Molybdenite, the main ore of molybdenum, occurs widely, but in small deposits. The term was first used for lead-bearing substances, and later its meaning was extended to include graphite and molybdenite. These two minerals are similar, but molybdenite has a higher specific gravity, a lighter bluish tinge and a brighter metallic lustre. It often occurs as scaly masses and the individual layers are easily bent. Molybdenite is used as a dry lubricant, which is resistant to high temperatures. Molybdenum is used to make hard, resistant steels, and also in the manufacture of tools, drills and electrical equipment.

Molybdenite with quartz and molybdite

Six-sided tabular crystals

Molybdenite in granitic rock

MOLYBDENITE

*Colour	bluish grey
Lustre	metallic
Transparency	opaque
Streak	lead-grey, greenish tint distinguishes it from graphite
*Hardness	1–1.5
Cleavage	perfect parallel to base; laminae are flexible but not elastic
*Tenacity	sectile and almost malleable
Habit	tabular crystals have a hexagonal outline; usually as leafy or scaly masses, also massive or granular
Specific gravity	4.7–4.8
*Other tests	greasy feel; leaves a bluish-grey mark on paper
Crystal system	hexagonal
Occurrence	usually found in granites, or sometimes diorites, in cavities, pegmatites or high-temperature pneumatolytic veins, associated with cassiterite, fluorite, scheelite and wolframite. Also of contact metamorphic origin occurring with garnet, pyroxenes, scheelite, pyrite and tourmaline
Examples	in quartz veins crossing granite in Colorado and New Jersey (USA); also in Australia, Bolivia, Italy and Norway

S tibnite, also known as antimonite, is the chief source of commercial antimony. It is widely distributed, but does not usually occur in large deposits. Stibnite is found mostly in low temperature hydrothermal veins, but also occurs as a replacement deposit and as a hot spring deposit. It may be associated with a variety of other minerals such as realgar, orpiment, galena, marcasite, pyrite, cinnabar and quartz. The largest deposits are in the Hunan Province of China, where stibnite occurs as veins and pockets in brecciated sandstone. The name is derived from the old Greek word for the mineral, *stibi*, meaning 'antimony'.

Acicular crystals

Stibnite

Prismatic crystals

STIBNITE

*Colour	steel-grey
*Lustre	metallic, may tarnish, sometimes iridescent on surface
Transparency	opaque
Streak	steel-grey
*Hardness	2
*Cleavage	perfect lengthwise
Fracture	subconchoidal; sectile; brittle but thin laminae slightly flexible
*Habit	elongated prismatic or needle-like crystals, striated along length, may be bent or twisted; radiating or sometimes granular
Specific gravity	4.5–4.6
Other tests	thin splinters melt in a flame colouring it greenish blue; powder soluble in concentrated hydrochloric acid; decomposes easily in potassium hydroxide solution staining it orange
Crystal system	orthorhombic
Alteration	alters to antimony oxides, e.g. red needle-like kermesite crystals or other yellow powdery minerals called antimony ochres
Occurrence	in veins associated with silver, lead and mercury minerals; also as a hot spring deposit with realgar, orpiment and cinnabar
Examples	China, Japan, Romania, Bolivia and Mexico

Rutile TiO_2

Rutile, an ore of titanium, is a high-temperature form of titanium dioxide. Low-temperature forms are *anatase* and *brookite*. Rutile is a primary mineral in igneous rocks and high-temperature metamorphic rocks. Because of its resistance to alteration, it occurs in placer deposits. Sands rich in rutile are worked in Australia. A well-known rutile-bearing granite occurs in Kragero, Norway. It is collected for its attractive twins and multiple intergrowths, though gem-quality crystals, found at Minas Gerais, Brazil, are extremely rare. Needle-like inclusions in rock-crystal (quartz), known as *sagenite* or *needle-stone*, make attractive polished specimens. Rutile disperses light six times as much as diamond; such 'fire' makes it easily detected. It is named from the Latin for 'golden red'.

Needles in quartz

Red adamantine crystals

Knee-shaped twin crystal

RUTILE

*Colour	reddish brown, sometimes yellow or black
*Lustre	adamantine, high dispersion can give 'fire'
Transparency	transparent when thin, most often translucent, occasionally opaque
Streak	pale brown
Hardness	6–6.5
Cleavage	prismatic, distinct
Fracture	conchoidal to uneven
*Habit	commonly needle-like, vertically striated crystals; sometimes granular, massive
*Twinning	common, often giving knee-shaped twins (see also cassiterite)
Specific gravity	4.2–4.3
Crystal system	tetragonal
Occurrence	accessory mineral in many plutonic igneous rocks, also eclogites; in some pegmatites, apatite and quartz veins; common accessory in gneisses and schists; in sands, clays and shales as a detrital mineral
Examples	in fissures in the Swiss Alps; Graves Mountain, Georgia and Nelson County, Virginia (USA). Sites in Australia, Brazil, Italy, Mexico and Norway

SnO_2 **Cassiterite**

C assiterite or tinstone is the only
abundant tin ore. The deposits in
Cornwall, England, were the main source
until the nineteenth century. It is one of
the few minerals that does not occur in
great quantities in the United States. A
concentrically banded form with a
fibrous structure is called *wood tin*, or
toad's eye when formed on a small scale.
Some gem-quality cassiterite occurs,
especially in Spain and Namibia, but most
is collected for the knee-shaped twins
that are common. Cassiterite has an
unusually high specific gravity for a non-
metallic mineral. This property, together
with its high resistance to weathering,
mean that cassiterite is often found in
stream and beach deposits. The name is
derived from the Greek
word for 'tin'. The main
uses for tin are in the
metal-plating industry
and in various
alloys.

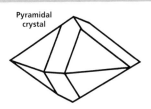

Pyramidal
crystal

Crystals

Crystals

CASSITERITE

Colour	brown to black
*Lustre	adamantine to submetallic, splendent
Transparency	translucent
*Streak	grey-white to brownish
Hardness	6–7
Cleavage	prismatic, imperfect
Fracture	subconchoidal to uneven; brittle
*Habit	short prismatic crystals, sometimes long with steep pyramidal ends; radially fibrous, concretionary masses (wood tin)
*Twinning	common, to give well-known 'knee-twins'
*Specific gravity	6.8–7.1 (to 6.1 for fibrous masses)
Crystal system	tetragonal
Occurrence	in high-temperature hydrothermal veins with quartz within and near to granites; the associated granite may be altered to a quartz-muscovite rock called greisen; associated minerals include mica, quartz, fluorite, wolframite, arsenopyrite, native bismuth, topaz and tourmaline; rounded pebbles are called stream tin
Examples	ore deposits in Malaysia, Indonesia, China, the former USSR, Bolivia; crystals in England and Germany

Cuprite Cu_2O

Cuprite, also known as red copper oxide, is an important copper ore, which occurs in large amounts as a secondary mineral in copper deposits. It resembles cinnabar and hematite in colour, but it can be distinguished by its hardness, which is between the two, and its streak. The fine, hair-like crystal form is called *chalcotrichite*. An earthy, reddish brown variety containing iron oxides is called the tile ore. Gem-quality cuprite, called *ruby copper*, is rare. The only sites containing stones suitable for cutting are Santa Rita, New Mexico, USA, and Onganyo, Namibia. The name is derived from the Latin *cuprum* meaning 'copper'.

Red, matted, acicular crystals

Cuprite

Crystals on calcite

CUPRITE

*Colour	red to very dark red
Lustre	submetallic to adamantine, or earthy
Transparency	subtranslucent, subtransparent when thin
*Streak	brownish red, shining
*Hardness	3.5–4
Cleavage	poor
Fracture	uneven, conchoidal; brittle
Habit	octahedral crystals, more rarely dodecahedra or cubes; sometimes in matted, straight hair-like crystals; massive or earthy
Specific gravity	5.8–6.1
Crystal system	cubic
Alteration	to malachite
Occurrence	common in the oxidized zone of copper deposits often accompanied by malachite, azurite, chalcocite and native copper
Examples	Redruth, Liskeard and the Lizard, Cornwall (England), Chessy near Lyon (France), Broken Hill, NSW (Australia), Bisbee, Arizona (USA), Tsumeb (Namibia)

Massive form

Lodestone attracting iron nail

Magnetite has a strongly magnetic character. People of early civilizations noticed that magnetized specimens, called *lodestones*, attracted other magnetic materials and, after swinging freely, aligned themselves in the Earth's magnetic field. Lodestone is found in Magnet Cove, Arkansas, USA. Magnetite grains can occur in detrital sediments, associated with corundum deposits. The magnetite can be extracted with a magnet. Magnetite is an important iron ore. Swedish magnetite, which is associated with iron silicates, produces an extremely hard steel.

MAGNETITE

*Colour	black
Lustre	metallic or submetallic to dull
Transparency	opaque
*Streak	black
Hardness	5.5–6.5
Cleavage	none, octahedral parting
Fracture	subconchoidal
Habit	octahedral crystals, less commonly dodecahedra; granular or massive
Twinning	common
Specific gravity	5.2
*Other tests	strongly magnetic
Crystal system	cubic
Occurrence	common; accessory in igneous rocks, in metamorphic rocks and high-temperature mineral veins; in detrital sediments and in iron-formations
Examples	large deposits are found in Scandinavia (e.g. Kiruna, Sweden), Bushveld (South Africa), Adirondacks (New York (USA) and the Ural Mountains (the former USSR); black sands are widespread in Alaska, California, Idaho, Montana, Colorado, Oregon and Washington (USA); beautiful crystals are found at Bolzano (Italy) and in Binnenthal (Switzerland)

Octahedral crystals

Hematite Fe_2O_3

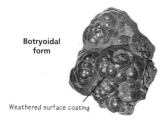

Botryoidal form

Weathered surface coating

Specular hematite

tabular crystals

metallic lustre

Botryoidal form

Hematite is named after the Greek word for blood. When earthy and mixed with clay minerals, it forms red ochre, which has long been used as a pigment. It is the leading iron ore, because it is both common and rich in iron. Varieties are *specularite* (a crystalline form with a bright metallic lustre), *kidney ore* (reniform masses), and *micaceous hematite* or *iron mica* (small shiny masses). Distinguishing features of hematite are the colour of its streak and its hardness, which makes it a useful polishing material, called *jeweller's rouge*. In ancient times hematite was used to stop bleeding, acting in a similar way to alum, which is used in styptic pencils. It is the most oxidized form of iron oxide and is a major constituent of rust.

HEMATITE

*Colour	steel-grey to iron-black, sometimes iridescent; dull to bright red when massive or earthy
Lustre	metallic, or dull and earthy
Transparency	opaque, translucent in thin pieces
*Streak	dark red to red-brown
*Hardness	5–6
Cleavage	none
Fracture	uneven; brittle
Habit	crystals tabular or rhombohedral, sometimes with curved or striated faces; sometimes arranged in rose-like form in 'iron roses'; massive, laminated or earthy, often mammilated or botryoidal
Twinning	common, to give striations
Specific gravity	4.9–5.3
Crystal system	trigonal
Occurrence	widely distributed; accessory mineral in igneous rocks, and in hydrothermal veins; formed under sedimentary conditions often as ooliths or as a cement, as a primary mineral; also as a secondary mineral on the weathering of iron-bearing minerals
Examples	Precambrian terrains in USA, Brazil, Australia, England; iron roses in Switzerland and Brazil

$FeCr_2O_4$ **Chromite**

Chromite always contains small quantities of magnesiochromite ($MgCr_2O_4$), spinel ($MgAl_2O_4$), and other spinels. Hence, the specific gravity of specimens varies considerably. Chromite is the only chromium ore. It is important in making steel alloys (especially stainless steel), chromium-plating, leather-tanning and paints. It is extremely resistant to high temperatures and is used to make bricks for lining blast furnaces. These bricks are usually made of crude chromite and coal tar. The brown streak and weaker magnetic character distinguish chromite from magnetite. Other useful distinguishing features are its insolubility in acids and its association with ultrabasic igneous rocks.

Massive form

Granular form

Aggregate of crystals

CHROMITE

*Colour	black to brownish black
Lustre	metallic to submetallic
Transparency	opaque, translucent in thin flakes
*Streak	dark brown
Hardness	5.5
Cleavage	none
Fracture	uneven; brittle
Habit	rarely octahedral crystals; commonly massive, granular
Specific gravity	4.1–5.1
*Other tests	weakly magnetic
Crystal system	cubic
Occurrence	accessory mineral in ultrabasic igneous rocks and serpentinites derived from them; may be concentrated into workable layers in such rocks; sometimes in alluvial sands and gravels
Examples	important countries for production are South Africa, the former USSR, Albania and Zimbabwe; also found in Montana (USA); good crystals occur in Namibia

Corundum Al_2O_3

Ruby

Corundum

The best known and prized varieties of this hard and durable mineral are *rubies* (red) and *sapphires* (blue). Yellow, green, and brown forms also occur. 'Star' sapphires and rubies are opalescent and display six- or three-pointed stars in reflected light, an effect called *asterism*, caused by minute rutile crystals. The price of high-quality gemstones can exceed that of diamonds. The presence of corundum in alluvial sands and gravels is due to the mineral's extreme hardness, which is second only to diamond, and durability. An impure form of corundum, called *emery*, is used as an abrasive.

Blue, barrel-shaped crystal in gneiss

CORUNDUM

Colour	very variable; can be blue, red, yellow, brown, green
Lustre	adamantine to vitreous
Transparency	transparent to translucent
Streak	white
***Hardness**	9
Cleavage	none, basal parting
Fracture	uneven to conchoidal
***Habit**	rough prisms or barrel-shaped crystals bounded by steep pyramids; faces show horizontal ridges and striations; also massive and granular, called emery (often with magnetite and spinel)
Twinning	common, often repeated, giving striations
***Specific gravity**	4
Crystal system	trigonal
Occurrence	accessory mineral in syenites and nepheline syenites; in contact metamorphosed shales and bauxite; in some feldspar pegmatites; in metamorphosed impure limestones; in river and placer deposits
Examples	Mogok (Myanmar), Sri Lanka, Madagascar, South Africa, Glebe Hill, Ardnamurchan (Scotland), Naxos Island (Greece), Turkey and the central Urals (the former USSR)

Spinel is not a single mineral, but it is used as the name for a series of minerals that contain varying amounts of magnesian spinel with iron, zinc and manganese, namely *hercynite* ($FeAl_2O_4$), *gahnite* ($ZnAl_2O_4$), and *galaxite* ($MnAl_2O_4$). Chromite may also be present. Gem-quality stones have long been prized, especially the red ruby spinel. Often mistaken for rubies and sapphires, spinel was collected in royal treasuries. The best known stone is the Timur Ruby in the British Crown jewels. Many spinels, like corundum, are now manufactured synthetically in large quantities. Red spinel turns brown or black on heating, changing to green, colourless and back to red on cooling.

Blue-black form with calcite and quartz

SPINEL

Colour	variable: colourless when pure, often red or blue, green, brown or black
Lustre	vitreous
Transparency	transparent to almost opaque
Streak	white or grey to brown
Hardness	7.5–8
Cleavage	none, octahedral parting
Fracture	conchoidal
*Habit	octahedral crystals, massive
*Twinning	common on octahedron ('spinel twins')
Specific gravity	3.5–4.1
Crystal system	cubic
Occurrence	accessory in igneous rocks (e.g. gabbro): in magnesium- and aluminium-rich contact metamorphosed dolomitic limestones and aluminous xenoliths in igneous rocks; in gravels due to its resistance to weathering and hardness
Examples	gem quality in Myanmar, Sri Lanka, India, Thailand, Madagascar and Afghanistan: good specimens at Monte Somma, Vesuvius (Italy), Orange County, New York and Sterling Hill Mine, Ogdensburg, New York (USA)

Ruby spinel

Ruby spinel

Single crystal

Pyrolusite MnO_2

Radiating habit

Crystals

Dendritic form

PYROLUSITE

*Colour	black or blue-black
Lustre	metallic to dull and earthy
Transparency	opaque
Streak	black to blue-black
Hardness	6–6.5 (1–2 when massive)
Cleavage	perfect, prismatic
Fracture	uneven; splintery
Habit	usually massive, often reniform, concretionary or powdery; forms dendritic (plant-like) markings on joint surfaces; crystals rare, well-formed prisms
Specific gravity	5.1 (crystals), 4.4–5 (massive)
Crystal system	tetragonal
Occurrence	in oxidized zone of manganese ore deposits, in bog or shallow water sediments, as nodules on the sea-bed and in quartz veins
Examples	found at Platten, Bavaria, (Germany), the former Czechoslovakia, Cornwall (England). Large deposits at Nikepol (Ukraine), Chiatura, Georgia, Deccan (India), Brazil, Cuba, Ghana, South Africa

Pyrolusite is an important ore of the metal manganese, which is used in steel-making, both to remove oxygen and sulphur, and as an alloying metal. Rare, well-formed crystals are called *polianite*. The massive form is by far the most abundant, the colour and the softness being the main diagnostic feature. The name comes from the Greek words meaning 'fire' and 'wash', referring to the fact that pyrolusite was once used to remove iron oxide discoloration in glass-making. Pyrolusite occurs as a constituent of the mixture of black hydrous manganese-bearing minerals known as *wad*, together with psilomelane and manganite.

Limonite nodule

Iridescent
stalactites

Goethite

GOETHITE

Colour	dark brown, but yellow when as fine-grained earthy varieties
Lustre	adamantine when crystalline, often silky when massive
Transparency	thin fragments transparent, opaque when massive
*Streak	yellow-brown
Hardness	5–5.5
Cleavage	one perfect
Fracture	uneven
Habit	crystals prismatic or scaly, but rare; usually massive with a radially fibrous structure as concretions, stalactites or botryoidal forms
Specific gravity	3.3 (massive)–4.3 (crystals)
Crystal system	orthorhombic
Occurrence	in limonite in weathered or hydrothermally altered iron-bearing rocks; as sediments in bogs at high latitudes and rarely precipitated in marine conditions at the outcrop of sulphide deposits
Examples	deposits in France, Canada, Germany and Cuba; crystals at Lostwithiel and Botallach, Cornwall (England), the former Czechoslovakia, the former USSR and the USA

G oethite forms attractive but rare
crystals. Common forms are
massive, with a radially fibrous structure.
It is found in large amounts as the
amorphous mineral assemblage called
limonite. Limonite is a blanket term for
all forms of hydrated ferric oxide, which
has been formed by the oxidation and
weathering of iron minerals. It includes
the famous yellow ochres associated with
iron deposits and used as pigments.
Limonite is distinguished from
crystalline goethite by its vitreous lustre
and lack of cleavage. Both have a
characteristic yellow-brown streak.
Goethite is deposited as a sediment in
bogs at high altitudes, where it forms *bog-iron ores*. It is named after the German
poet J.W. von Goethe, who collected
minerals.

Ilmenite $FeTiO_3$

Ilmenite, an ore of titanium, is a black mineral with a metallic lustre when pure. It can contain varying amounts of the related magnesian mineral *giekielite* ($MgTiO_3$), which affects its physical properties. The variety *menaccanite*, found at Menaccan Sands, Cornwall, England, was one of the first reported descriptions of ilmenite. The occurrence of ilmenite in sands reflects its high resistance to weathering. In magmas, it is prone to segregate with magnetite or hematite, because of its relatively high specific gravity. It is distinguished from hematite by its streak, and from magnetite by its non-magnetic nature.

Ilmenite with feldspar

ILMENITE

Colour	black
Lustre	metallic to submetallic
Transparency	opaque
***Streak**	black to brownish black
Hardness	5–6
Cleavage	none, basal partings
Fracture	conchoidal
Habit	thick tabular crystals; massive, compact; disseminated grains in basic igneous rocks
Twinning	common
Specific gravity	4.5–5
***Other tests**	non-magnetic
Crystal system	trigonal
Occurrence	common accessory as grains in basic igneous rocks, such as gabbros and diorites; larger amounts as ilmenite-magnetite or ilmenite-hematite segregations in gabbros and anorthosites; it is concentrated in some beach sands, alongside magnetite, rutile and monazite; less commonly in quartz veins and pegmatites
Examples	Egersund (Norway), Taberg (Sweden), Alland Lake, (Canada) and Adirondacks, (USA). Large deposits in India, Brazil and former USSR. Beach placer deposits in India.

Single crystal

metallic lustre

Tabular crystals

Granular form

cubic cleavage

White cubic crystals

H alite, or rock salt, is best known as common table salt. It occurs within thick, stratified evaporite deposits and in domes. These deposits form when layers of light, plastic halite are compressed and rise up through overlying layers of sediment. Halite is formed where enclosed bodies of seawater evaporate, and the different salts separate out in layers, as in the Permian evaporites of Stassfurt, Germany. Apart from its use in the preparation of food, halite is the main source of chlorine used in the manufacture of household bleach. By-products include potassium, magnesium, bromine and iodine.

Cubic crystals

HALITE

Colour	colourless or white when pure, often yellow or red, sometimes with blue or purple tints
Lustre	vitreous
Transparency	transparent to translucent
Streak	white
Hardness	2–2.5
Cleavage	perfect cubic
Fracture	conchoidal; brittle
Habit	often as masses of interlocking cubic crystals, occasionally as octahedra; cubes with hollow faces are known as hopper crystals; also massive and granular
Specific gravity	2.2
*Other tests	salty, soluble in water; colours a flame bright yellow
Crystal system	cubic
Occurrence	as a precipitate in sedimentary deposits, sometimes interbedded with clay, and characteristically associated with other evaporites (sylvite, gypsum and anhydrite) and with dolomite; also as a direct sublimate from volcanic exhalations
Examples	Cheshire (England), Lorraine (France), Salzburg (Austria), New York, Michigan and Ohio (USA)

Fluorite CaF_2

Octahedron

Blue John

Radiating crystals

Cubic crystals with
bands of colour

FLUORITE

Colour	variable; colourless when pure, tinted by impurities to blue, pink, purple, green or yellow
*Lustre	vitreous
Transparency	transparent to translucent
Streak	white
Hardness	4
*Cleavage	parallel to octahedron
Fracture	conchoidal to uneven; brittle
Habit	crystals common, as cubes or octahedra; compact, or coarsely or finely granular
Twinning	interpenetrant twins typical
Specific gravity	3–3.3
Other tests	soluble in concentrated sulphuric acid, giving off fumes of hydrofluoric acid; often strongly fluorescent under ultraviolet light; when heated to temperatures above 100°C (212°F), emits light in darkness
Crystal system	cubic
Occurrence	found in sulphide deposits as gangue with barytes and quartz; sometimes found in pegmatites; can also form from saline waters in enclosed basins
Examples	England, Italy, Switzerland, Norway, Canada, the USA, and the former USSR

The best known type of fluorite is Blue John, a violet-blue and white or yellowish banded variety used in jewellery and vases. Miners once called the beautifully coloured crystals 'ore flowers'. It is a widely distributed mineral and is now mined in vast quantities. It is an important raw material used to prepare several fluorine compounds, such as hydrofluoric acid. It is also used in the manufacture of pottery, in the optical and plastics industries, and in the metallurgical treatment of bauxite. Lower grade fluorite is used as a flux in steel-making and foundry work. Its name comes from the Latin *fluere*, meaning 'to flow', which refers to its use as a flux. It is also known as fluorspar.

S ylvite, or sylvine, is often associated with halite, but is much less common, because the potassium ions are retained by clay minerals rather than being dissolved in water. Sylvite also resembles halite, but it is less dense, has a more bitter taste, and is less brittle, deforming readily under pressure. It may be reddish because of disseminated hematite, or purple due to exposure to natural radiation. It is used as a fertilizer, either directly or in the preparation of potassium salts. The deposits at Saskatchewan, Canada are over 900m (2950ft) deep and form the world's most important resources. The name sylvite comes from the early chemical name for the salt *sal digestiva sylvii*, after the German anatomist Franciscus Sylvius.

Cupriferous form

Crystals on halite

Sylvite

SYLVITE

Colour	colourless or white, bluish or yellowish red
Lustre	vitreous
Transparency	transparent when pure
Streak	white
Hardness	2
Cleavage	perfect cubic
Fracture	uneven; less brittle than halite
Habit	rare cubic crystals, modified by octahedron; more commonly granular crystalline masses
Specific gravity	2
*Other tests	salty, more bitter than halite; soluble in water; colours a flame red; not as deliquescent as halite
Crystal system	cubic
Occurrence	associated with halite and carnallite, occurring as a saline residue in Stassfurt (Germany) and other salt deposits; also around fumaroles of volcanoes, e.g. Vesuvius (Italy)
Examples	Stassfurt (Germany), Etna and Vesuvius (Italy), Kalusz (Poland), Saskatchewan (Canada), Utah, Texas and New Mexico (USA)

Calcite $CaCO_3$

Calcite is a major rock-forming mineral. It is the principal component of limestones, other calcareous sedimentary rocks and marble. The calcite in limestones may originate as an accumulation of shells or as a precipitate. Other calcite precipitates are travertine and tufa – the former in stalactites and stalagmites. It is also a common gangue mineral in hydrothermal veins. The large clear crystals of the variety *Iceland spar* display double refraction – that is, when placed on a sheet of paper marked with a spot, two spots are seen, and, on revolving the crystal, one spot remains still, while the other appears to revolve around it. Limestones are quarried to produce lime for cement. This process is energy-intensive, because the rock has to be heated to high temperatures in order to decompose calcite into carbon dioxide (CO_2) and lime (CaO).

Nail-head spar

Barrel-shaped crystals

Stalactitic form

CALCITE

Colour	usually colourless or white, may be brown, red, blue, green or black
Lustre	vitreous, somewhat pearly on cleavages
Transparency	transparent to translucent, almost opaque when deeply coloured
Streak	white
Hardness	3
*Cleavage	rhombohedral, perfect
Fracture	conchoidal, but rare due to perfect cleavage
Habit	very variable; commonly flat rhombohedra; prisms topped with rhombohedra form nail-head spar; steep scalenohedra form dog-tooth spar; aggregates are fibrous, granular, massive or stalactitic
Twinning	common
Specific gravity	2.7
Other tests	effervesces readily and dissolves in cold, dilute hydrochloric acid
Crystal system	trigonal
Occurrence	a widespread rock-forming mineral; in sedimentary rocks, such as limestones, and in metamorphic rocks, such as marble
Examples	large clear prisms in Iceland, Germany and USA; dog-tooth spar in England

Acicular crystals

Pseudohexagonal twinned crystals

Flos-ferri

ARAGONITE

Colour	colourless to white, or yellowish
Lustre	vitreous
Transparency	transparent to translucent
Streak	white
Hardness	3.5–4
Cleavage	poor
Fracture	subconchoidal
*Habit	stout, prismatic, twinned crystals with a pseudo-hexagonal symmetry are most common; untwinned crystals rare; stalactitic and encrusting masses with a fibrous structure
Twinning	very common
Specific gravity	2.9
*Other tests	soluble with effervescence in dilute hydrochloric acid
Crystal system	orthorhombic
Occurrence	less widespread than calcite; deposited from hot springs or in caves; in veins and cavities with calcite and dolomite; as the nacreous shell on many molluscs and in pearls
Examples	Molina de Aragon (Spain), Fort Collins, Colorado (USA), Bastennes (France), Alston Moor, Cumberland (England)

Aragonite is a polymorph of the more common calcite. (Polymorphs are substances with the same chemical composition, but with different properties.) Aragonite is unstable when exposed to high temperatures and pressures. As a result, fossil mollusc shells originally made of aragonite are now of calcite. Although unstable, aragonite can be produced by biological action or by precipitation under the right conditions of temperature, or in the presence of dissolved metals, such as lead, strontium or zinc. It is distinguished from calcite by its fibrous, rounded form, its lack of distinct rhombohedral cleavage, and a higher specific gravity. Aragonite is used as an ornamental stone. A popular banded variety is called *onyx* or *onyx marble. Flos-ferri* consists of slender, intertwined branches.

Dolomite $CaMg(CO_3)_2$

Dolomite is similar to calcite and accompanies it in many limestones. It usually occurs as a secondary mineral, formed by the reaction of magnesium-bearing fluids seeping through limestones. The variety *pearl spar* is white, grey or pale brown, with a pearly lustre, while *brown*, *rhomb* or *bitter-spar* are iron-bearing varieties, coloured brown by the presence of *ankerite*, a cross between dolomite and siderite. The faces of dolomite crystals are often curved, sometimes so acutely that the crystals become saddle-shaped. Dolomitic rocks are useful building materials and refractories (materials that can withstand high temperatures). Dolomite, a source of magnesium and fluxes in the steel industry, is distinguished from calcite by its reluctance to dissolve in dilute acid.

Aggregate of pink crystal

overlapping scales

Aggregate of yellowish crystal

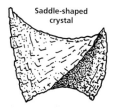

Saddle-shaped crystal

DOLOMITE

Colour	colourless, or white to cream and yellow brown; sometimes pale pink
Lustre	vitreous
Transparency	translucent
Streak	white
Hardness	3.5–4
Cleavage	rhombohedral, perfect
Fracture	subconchoidal
Habit	rhombohedral crystals with curved faces, often composed of overlapping scales; massive, granular
Twinning	common
Specific gravity	2.8–2.9
*Other tests	slowly dissolves with effervescence in cold, dilute hydrochloric acid, readily on warming
Crystal system	trigonal
Alteration	weathers brown
Occurrence	rock-forming mineral in dolomitic limestones, usually secondary; widespread gangue mineral in hydrothermal veins, especially accompanying galena and sphalerite
Examples	Brosso and Traversella, Piedmont (Italy), Binnenthal (Switzerland), the Freiberg and Schneeberg Mines (Germany), Cornwall (England), Joplin, Missouri (USA)

Unlike calcite and dolomite, magnesite does not usually form sedimentary rocks. Instead, it occurs as an alteration product of magnesian mineral-bearing rocks by water containing carbonic acid, or of carbonate-bearing rocks by water containing dissolved magnesium. Magnesite usually occurs as a replacement deposit in carbonaceous rocks. The white massive variety can have a porcelain-like appearance resembling chert due to the presence of opal. An important ore of magnesium, it is heated to drive off carbon dioxide leaving magnesium oxide (MgO), which is used in making refractory bricks and furnace linings, special cements, and in the paper industry. It has been used as an antacid for digestive disorders.

Crystals

Magnesite

porcellaneous lustre

Massive chalk-like form

MAGNESITE

*Colour	white or colourless, often discoloured greyish or yellowish brown
Lustre	vitreous, or dull when compact
Transparency	transparent to translucent
Streak	white
Hardness	3.5–4.5
*Cleavage	rhombohedral, perfect
Fracture	conchoidal
Habit	crystals rare and usually rhombohedral; massive, granular, fibrous or compact porcellaneous and chalk-like
Specific gravity	3 (up to 3.2 with iron present)
*Other tests	little reaction with cold dilute hydrochloric acid, dissolves with effervescence on warming
Crystal system	trigonal
Occurrence	uncommon; alteration product of peridotites alongside talc and serpentine; replacement mineral in dolomites and limestones
Examples	Euboea and Macedonia (Greece), Styria (Austria), the Ural Mountains (the former USSR), Manchuria, Korea, Quebec (Canada), Paradise Mountains, Nevada (USA)

Siderite $FeCO_3$

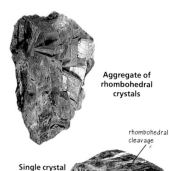

Aggregate of rhombohedral crystals

rhombohedral cleavage

Single crystal

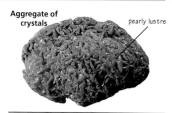

Aggregate of crystals

pearly lustre

S iderite is a major source of iron for steel making, because it is easily worked, often free of sulphur and phosphorus, and sometimes manganese-rich. Its colour and higher specific gravity distinguish it from calcite and dolomite, and its rhombohedral cleavage, from sphalerite. It occurs in the Coal Measures as beds and nodules of impure iron carbonate called *clay ironstone*, which used to be a valuable iron ore. A dark carbonaceous variety is called *blackband*. *Oolitic ironstone* is formed most often by the same colloidal processes that form oolitic limestones. Less commonly, iron-rich fluids form siderite as a secondary mineral in calcareous rocks. When extensive, these deposits are economically important. Siderite is also known as chalybite, named after the *Chalybes*, ancient iron workers who lived by the Black Sea.

SIDERITE

*Colour	brown, yellowish brown, grey-brown
Lustre	vitreous, inclining to pearly on cleavages
Transparency	transparent to translucent
Streak	white
Hardness	3.5–4.5
*Cleavage	rhombohedral, perfect
Fracture	uneven
*Habit	rhombohedral crystals often with curved faces made up of overlapping scales; massive, granular or concretionary
Twinning	common, often lamellar
*Specific gravity	4 (to 3.8 when magnesium is present)
*Other tests	dissolves slowly with effervescence in cold dilute hydrochloric acid, readily on warming
Crystal system	trigonal
Occurrence	widespread massive siderite deposits in sedimentary rocks, especially in clays and shales as concretions; gangue mineral in hydrothermal veins with pyrite and galena; as bog-iron ore in high latitude lakes and swamps
Examples	Mesozoic rocks in England, Belgium, Luxemburg and France; large deposits in Pennsylvania (USA) and in veins in central Germany

Malachite has long been prized as a semi-precious stone. Beautiful ornaments and table tops are made from banded forms of malachite. It was popular among the ancient Greeks and Romans, and it later became fashionable in the courts of the Russian Czars. Malachite is also a copper ore. One major deposit is at Shaba (formerly Katanga) province, Zaire. Crushed malachite has been used as a pigment. It is known as green copper carbonate, in contrast to azurite, known as blue copper carbonate. Malachite is named after the Greek for 'mallow', as it is similar in colour to a mallow leaf.

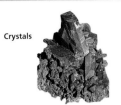

Crystals

MALACHITE

*Colour	bright green
Lustre	fibrous aggregates silky to dull; crystals adamantine
Transparency	translucent
Streak	pale green
Hardness	3.5–4
Cleavage	perfect
Fracture	subconchoidal or uneven
*Habit	mammillated or botryoidal form with concentric bands and fibrous structure; crystals rare, tufts of twinned needles and prisms
Twinning	common
Specific gravity	3.9–4
*Other tests	soluble with effervescence in dilute hydrochloric acid
Crystal system	monoclinic
Occurrence	widespread in the oxidized zone of copper deposits as a secondary mineral, associated with azurite, cuprite, native copper, limonite and chrysocolla
Examples	large masses in the Shaba Province (Zaire); Demidoff Mine, Nizhne-Tagilisk and Sverdlovsk (the former USSR), for large masses; good crystals at Betzdorf (Germany), Chessy (France), Redruth, Cornwall (England) Copper Queen Mine, Bisbee, Arizona (USA)

Botryoidal form

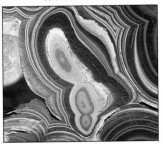

Colour-banded form

Azurite $Cu_3(CO_3)(OH)_2$

A zurite is named after the Persian word for blue. Its attractive blue colour has made it a semi-precious stone, although its softness has limited its use. Unlike malachite, it does not occur in sufficiently large compact masses to feature widely for ornamental purposes. It was used in ancient times in Asia to make blue paints for murals and it is still used as a pigment today. An attractive stone called *azurmalachite* is an interbanded form of azurite and malachite. A popular form occurs at Copper Queen Mine, Bisbee, Arizona, USA. Fine crystals of azurite are found at Chessy, near Lyon, France, hence the alternative name chessylite.

Crystals of azurite with green malachite

Azurite

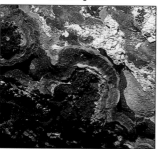

Aggregate of azurite with malachite

Encrusting form

AZURITE

*Colour	azure-blue, paler when earthy, darker in crystals
Lustre	vitreous to adamantine
Transparency	transparent to translucent
Streak	light blue
Hardness	3.5–4
Cleavage	good
Fracture	conchoidal
Habit	crystals either tabular or short prismatic, often complex and malformed; as radiating aggregates; also dull and earthy
Specific gravity	3.8
Twinning	rare
*Other tests	soluble with effervescence in dilute hydrochloric acid
Crystal system	monoclinic
Alteration	to malachite
Occurrence	as a secondary mineral in the oxidized zone of copper deposits along with malachite and its associated minerals; less widely distributed than malachite
Examples	fine crystals at Chessy (France), Tsumeb (Namibia), Bisbee, Arizona (USA), Redruth, Cornwall (England), Laurium (Greece), Romania, Siberia

W hen available in sufficient
quantities, witherite is an ore of
barium. It is used in speciality glasses
and for producing finely divided barium
sulphate. It was named after a
seventeenth-century mineralogist W.
Withering, who discovered it. Witherite
is always twinned, forming
pseudohexagonal pyramids. These often
show deep horizontal striations, giving
the appearance of a stack of pyramids. It
is distinguished from its close relative
strontianite by a flame test, which shows
green for witherite but crimson for
strontianite. Like other barium-
containing minerals, it is fairly dense (see
baryte). It is found
mainly as a gangue
mineral in lead-
zinc ore fields.

Radiating form

WITHERITE

Colour	colourless to grey, or pale yellow to brown
Lustre	vitreous, resinous on fracture surfaces
Transparency	transparent to translucent
Streak	white
Hardness	3–3.5
Cleavage	distinct
Fracture	uneven
Habit	crystals always twinned with pseudo-hexagonal form, deep horizontal striations sometimes making them look like a stack of pyramids; massive, granular, columnar, botryoidal
Twinning	ubiquitous
*Specific gravity	4.3
*Other tests	dissolves with effervescence in dilute hydrochloric acid; gives green flame test; may fluoresce or phosphoresce in ultraviolet light
Crystal system	orthorhombic
Occurrence	uncommon; in low-temperature hydrothermal veins with barytes, galena and anglesite
Examples	good crystals at Alston Moor, Cumberland and Hexham, Northumberland, (England) and Rosiclaire, Illinois (USA); masses at El Portal, California (USA) and Siberia (Russia)

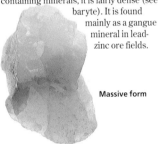

Massive form

Twinned crystals

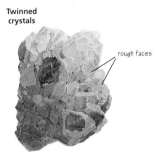

rough faces

Smithsonite $ZnCO_3$

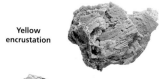

Yellow encrustation

White encrustation

Smithsonite

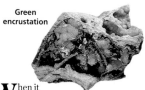

Green encrustation

When it has good colouring (especially translucent green) or banding, smithsonite, an ore of zinc, is used as an ornamental stone. The yellow variety contains cadmium and is known as *turkey-fat ore*. Smithsonite is produced by the action of water rich in zinc salts on carbonate rocks. The salt is usually zinc sulphate, which is produced by the oxidation of sphalerite (zinc sulphide). Smithsonite used to be called calamine, though this name is now generally used for a pink powder used in lotions and ointments. This powder is a mixture of smithsonite and zinc silicates. Smithsonite is named after James Smithson (1765–1829), the British mineralogist who founded the world-famous Smithsonian Institution in Washington DC.

SMITHSONITE

Colour	greyish white to shades of grey or brown; also apple green to bluish green
Lustre	vitreous
Transparency	translucent
Streak	white
Hardness	4–4.5
***Cleavage**	rhombohedral, perfect
Fracture	uneven
Habit	rhombohedral crystals with rough, curved faces, uncommon; massive in botryoidal, reniform or stalactitic encrustations
***Specific gravity**	4.4–4.5
***Other tests**	dissolves with effervescence in dilute hydrochloric acid
Crystal system	trigonal
Occurrence	secondary mineral in the oxidized zone of hydrothermal veins derived from primary sulphides, particularly sphalerite; often associated with malachite, azurite, cerussite, anglesite, pyromorphite and mimetite
Examples	Cumberland and Somerset, (England), Lanarkshire (Scotland), Colorado (USA), Kazakhstan (Russia), Tsumeb (Namibia), Santander (Spain), Attiki (Greece), Sardinia

B aryte is also known as barytes, barite, and heavy spar, because of its high density. In fact, the term baryte comes from the Greek word *baros* which means 'heavy'. Baryte is used in the manufacture of paint and paper, and is the greatest single source of the metallic element barium. Large amounts of baryte are used in the oil industry to make drilling muds. Baryte is often found in a fairly pure state with other gangue minerals (mining waste), such as calcite, fluorite and quartz, in deposits of metal ores, especially those of lead and zinc. Roseate clusters of baryte crystals, found as concretions in some sandstones in Oklahoma and Kansas, are called 'desert roses', the same name given for similar features formed from gypsum.

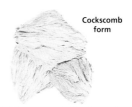

Cockscomb form

Tabular crystals

Thin, tabular crystals

BARYTE

Colour	colourless to white, often tinged with other colours, commonly yellow, red and brown, sometimes bluish
Lustre	vitreous, pearly on cleavage
Transparency	transparent to translucent
Streak	colourless
Hardness	3–3.5
*Cleavage	perfect parallel to base plane, good parallel to prism faces
Fracture	uneven; brittle
*Habit	tabular, sometimes prismatic when crystalline; often massive; sometimes fibrous or lamellar in clusters, or granular and stalagmitic
Twinning	uncommon
*Specific gravity	4.3–4.6
*Other tests	gives yellow-green flame test; insoluble in water or hydrochloric acid
Crystal system	orthorhombic
Occurrence	in veins and as a gangue mineral in ore deposits of lead, copper, zinc, silver, iron and nickel; as veins and nodules in limestones and marls; forms a cement in some sandstones
Examples	crystals up to 1 m (3.3 ft) found in England, the former Czechoslovakia, Romania and Germany

79

Gypsum $CaSO_4.2H_2O$

Gypsum is the most common sulphate mineral. It is usually the first evaporite mineral to be precipitated from water due to its poor solubility. Varieties include *selenite*, which is colourless and transparent, *satin spar*, the fibrous form, and *alabaster*, used for ornaments, which is massive and granular. Gypsum 'desert roses' are formed of interpenetrating platy crystals enclosing sand grains. These popular collectors' items are found in Morocco, Tunisia and the USA, in Arizona and New Mexico. Gypsum is used in plasters, including plaster of Paris, in fertilizers, and as a filler in such materials as crayons, paints and paper.

Aggregate of crystals

Crystals of selenite

Desert rose

GYPSUM

Colour	colourless or white, shades of grey, yellow or pink
Lustre	vitreous, pearly on cleavage faces
Transparency	transparent to translucent
Streak	white
***Hardness**	2 (easily scratched with a fingernail)
***Cleavage**	one perfect, two good, giving rhomb-shaped fragments
Habit	simple tabular crystals, often with curved faces; rosette-like aggregates and fibrous or granular masses
Twinning	'swallow-tail' contact twins common
Specific gravity	2.3
Other tests	flakes are somewhat flexible; dissolves in warm, dilute hydrochloric acid
Crystal system	monoclinic
Alteration	to and from anhydrite
Occurrence	in bedded deposits with other evaporites; important cap-rock on salt domes; small amounts in volcanic areas where sulphuric acid (from pyrite decay) reacts with limestones
Examples	widespread but including Germany, France, Canada, USA, the former USSR, Mexico and Italy

Massive form

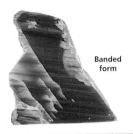

Banded form

A nhydrite is the form of calcium sulphate containing no water in its crystal structure. (Gypsum is the hydrated form.) In fact, its name is derived from the Greek *anhydras*, meaning 'without water'. Anhydrite is an evaporite mineral deposited from seawater at temperatures above 42°C (108°F). It is also formed when gypsum is dehydrated by a rise in temperature following burial. The reverse process, by which anhydrite is altered to become gypsum, occurs when anhydrite is exposed to water and cooler temperatures. Not surprisingly, anhydrite has much the same uses as gypsum. It is used as a source of sulphuric acid and as a filler in paper, and in various plasters. Treated with ammonia, it produces ammonium sulphate fertilizer. As with gypsum, the name anydrite can be used for the rock in evaporite deposits as well as the mineral. Rock anhydrite is used as polished slabs for interior facing. Anhydrite and gypsum will turn a flame brick-red due to the calcium present.

ANHYDRITE

Colour	colourless to bluish when transparent; white, pink or mauve when massive; often discoloured by impurities
Lustre	vitreous to pearly
Transparency	transparent to translucent
Streak	white
*Hardness	3–3.5
*Cleavage	three good cleavages at right angles
Fracture	uneven; splintery
Habit	usually massive and granular, but can be fibrous or lamellar; crystals rare
Twinning	common
*Specific gravity	2.9–3 (higher than calcite)
Crystal system	orthorhombic
Alteration	hydrates to gypsum
Occurrence	forms stratified bodies in the lower parts of evaporite deposits; abundant in cap-rock of salt domes; smaller amounts in hydrothermal veins and vesicles in igneous rocks
Examples	as caps to salt domes in Louisiana and Texas (USA); in stratified salt deposits in Stassfurt (Germany), Paris basin (France), Poland, Austria and India; purple crystals at Bex (Switzerland)

Celestine $SrSO_4$

Tabular crystals

Celestine, the chief ore of strontium, got its name from the Latin word for 'celestial', after the beautiful pale blue colour shown by some of its finest crystals. Strontium and its salts are used in fireworks and flares to impart a strong crimson colour. The crimson colouration of the flame is one of the tests used for identifying strontium salts. White crystals weighing 2–3 kg (4–7 lb) and measuring 50–75 cm (20–30 in) are found at Put-in-Bay, Ohio, USA. Strontium and the mineral strontianite ($SrCO_3$) are named after Strontian in Argyllshire, Scotland. Celestine is also known as celestite.

CELESTINE

Colour	colourless to pale blue
Lustre	vitreous, pearly on cleavage
Transparency	transparent to translucent
Streak	white
Hardness	3–3.5
*Cleavage	basal, perfect; prismatic, good
Fracture	imperfectly conchoidal; very brittle
Habit	tabular or prismatic crystals; may be fibrous or granular
*Specific gravity	3.9–4
*Other tests	insoluble in acids; gives crimson flame test; may fluoresce under ultraviolet light
Crystal system	orthorhombic
Occurrence	in sediments associated with sulphur; with evaporite minerals – gypsum, anhydrite and halite; gangue mineral in hydrothermal veins with galena and sphalerite; as concretions in clay and marl, in cavities in basic lavas and in the cap-rock of salt domes
Examples	bluish crystals in England and in gypsum and sulphur deposits in Italy; large crystals found in the USA; in basalt cavities in Italy and in pegmatites in Bohemia and Madagascar

pyramid faces

Prismatic crystals

Adamantine crystals

Greyish-white opaque crystals

ANGLESITE

Colour	colourless to white; may be tinged yellow, grey or blue
*Lustre	adamantine, sometimes resinous
Transparency	transparent to translucent
Streak	white
Hardness	2.5–3
Cleavage	basal, perfect; prismatic, distinct
Fracture	conchoidal; brittle
Habit	crystals often found prismatic, tabular or pyramidal; massive, compact and granular
*Specific gravity	6.2–6.4
Other tests	often yellow fluorescence under ultraviolet light; dissolves slowly in dilute nitric acid
Crystal system	orthorhombic
Occurrence	common in the oxidized zone of lead deposits in association with galena; as granular aggregates surrounding a core of galena; very rarely as a sublimate from volcanic activity
Examples	most famous are Broken Hill, NSW, (Australia) and Tsumeb (Namibia); others found in England, Scotland, Germany, USA and Mexico

This important lead ore was first found at Porys Mine on the island of Anglesey, Wales, after which it is named. Like most lead minerals, it has a high specific gravity. It is a secondary mineral, formed most often by the oxidation of a primary deposit of galena. It may occur as granular aggregates surrounding a core of galena, with concentric layers of anglesite identifiable by slight colour changes. Anglesite is often associated with other minerals, especially cerussite, copper carbonates, copper oxides, mimetite and pyromorphite. It can be distinguished from the carbonate mineral cerussite ($PbCO_3$) by the lack of reaction as it dissolves in nitric acid. Fine crystals come from Tsumeb, Namibia, Musen, Germany, and the Wheatley mine, Phoenixville, Pennsylvania, USA. The rare black, white and yellow prismatic crystals from Monteponi, Sardinia are famous among collectors. Because of its toxicity and discoloration, lead sulphate has been replaced by titanium oxide as a white pigment in paint.

83

Scheelite $CaWO_4$

Wolframite

Scheelite is an important ore of tungsten, especially in the USA. Tungsten is used to harden steels for use in high-speed tools and engine components, and to prepare tungsten carbides, abrasives which are second only to diamonds in hardness. Metallic tungsten has a high melting point – 3410°C (6170°F) – and is used in lamp filaments and spark plugs. Scheelite is named after K.W. Scheele, the eighteenth century Swedish chemist who discovered tungsten. Occurring alongside scheelite in high temperature veins and pegmatites is the related mineral wolframite $(Fe,Mn)WO_4$. Wolframite is a grey-black to brownish black, monoclinic mineral of high specific gravity (7–7.5) which shows one good cleavage. Outside the USA it is the principal ore of tungsten. The name wolframite comes from the German word *wolfram*, meaning 'tungsten'. Scheelite can be confused with quartz, with which it is commonly associated, but is distinguished by the characteristic electric blue to yellow fluorescence under ultraviolet light.

Scheelite in calcite

SCHEELITE

*Colour	yellowish white to brownish
Lustre	adamantine or vitreous
Transparency	transparent to opaque
Streak	white
Hardness	4.5–5
Cleavage	good, parallel to pyramid
Fracture	conchoidal to uneven; brittle
*Habit	small pyramidal crystals, also massive, granular or columnar
Twinning	penetration twins, common
*Specific gravity	5.9–6.1
Other tests	fluorescence bluish white in ultraviolet light; thermoluminescent
Crystal system	tetragonal
Occurrence	a high-temperature mineral found in quartz veins and greisens close to granites; associated with wolframite, cassiterite, molybdenite, mica, fluorite, topaz etc; in contact metamorphosed limestones with garnet, vesuvianite, sphene, hornblende and epidote
Examples	Carrock Mine England; in contact metamorphosed limestones in USA; in low-temperature veins in Canada, Australia and USA

Apatite crystals on calcite

Hexagonal crystal

Apatite is a widely distributed mineral occurring as fluorapatite (F), chloroapatite (Cl) and hydroxylapatite (OH). Its name comes from the Greek *apatao*, meaning 'deceit', because it may be mistaken for other minerals. It is distinguished from beryl and quartz by its lustre and lower hardness. Clear, well-coloured apatites are sometimes used as gemstones, such as 'asparagus stones', but they are rather soft. Apatite is the main constituent of bones and teeth, and in fluorine-bearing forms, is resistant to decay, which is why drinking water is fluoridized. Apatite is used in the manufacture of fertilizers and in the chemical industry.

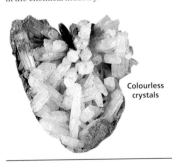

Colourless crystals

APATITE

Colour	sea-green or bluish green, yellow, brown, violet
*Lustre	vitreous to sub-resinous
Transparency	transparent to opaque
Streak	white
*Hardness	5
Cleavage	basal, very poor
Fracture	conchoidal or uneven; brittle
Habit	usually in prismatic or needle-like crystals, sometimes tabular; also massive, mammillated or concretionary
Specific gravity	3.2
Other tests	fluorescent under ultraviolet light, in brown, orange, or yellow; may phosphoresce and thermoluminesce; soluble in hydrochloric acid
*Crystal system	hexagonal
Occurrence	a common accessory mineral in rocks; occurs as large crystals in pegmatites; extensive deposits of phosphate rock may be interbedded with other sedimentary rocks
Examples	good crystals in Canada, Austria, Mexico, the former USSR, Uganda, Sweden; sedimentary phosphates important in the USA, Egypt, Morocco and Tunisia

Turquoise $CuAl_6(PO_4)_4(OH)_8.5H_2O$

Turquoise is a semi-precious blue gemstone. It is often mottled, with brown or black veinlets. It can be distinguished from the mineral crysocolla by its greater hardness. Care must be taken when handling it, because specimens can alter to an unattractive green if heated too much – due to friction when polishing – or on exposure to sunlight. It is also sensitive to soap, water and grease. Turquoise was used in Ancient Egyptian jewellery. American Indians also used it, typically in silver jewellery. Its name comes from the French *pierre turquoise*, meaning 'Turkish stone'. It was so called because it was brought into Europe via Turkey.

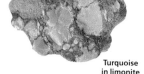

Turquoise in limonite

Turquoise

Turquoise

TURQUOISE

*Colour	sky-blue or blue-green
Lustre	crystals, vitreous; waxy when massive
Transparency	almost opaque
Streak	white or pale greenish
Hardness	5–6
Cleavage	good
Fracture	conchoidal
Habit	crystals rare and very small; usually massive in veins, concretions or encrustations
Specific gravity	2.6–2.8
Crystal system	triclinic
Occurrence	secondary mineral in veins and pockets in aluminium-rich rocks, often igneous which have undergone considerable alterations, usually in arid regions
Examples	Kuh-i-Nishapur, Neyshabur (Iran), Queensland, Victoria and New South Wales (Australia), River Umba Valley (Tanzania), Los Cerillos, New Mexico, and Nevada (USA)

Willemite and franklinite

franklinite

Willemite is a valuable ore of zinc. It is mined at Franklin Furnace, New Jersey, USA where it occurs in a crystalline limestone. At this locality it is associated with two other zinc minerals – zincite and franklinite – which are virtually restricted to this deposit. Zincite (ZnO) is deep red to orange-yellow in colour, with an orange-yellow streak. Franklinite ((Zn,Fe,Mn) (Fe,Mn)₂O₄) is iron black and is usually identified by its association with willemite and zincite. Willemite shows a characteristic strong green fluorescence under ultraviolet light. A manganese-bearing variety is called *troostite*. Willemite was named after King Willem Frederik I of the Netherlands.

Troostite in marble

Green willemite in calcite

calcite

WILLEMITE

*Colour	greenish yellow usual, can be brown or nearly white when pure
Lustre	vitreous to resinous
Transparency	transparent to almost opaque
Hardness	5.5
Cleavage	two imperfect cleavages
Fracture	uneven
Habit	prismatic crystals. Usually massive, granular
Specific gravity	4–4.1
*Other tests	usually strongly fluorescent under ultraviolet light
Crystal system	trigonal
Occurrence	found in crystalline limestone, possibly forming from the metamorphism of smithsonite or hemimorphite, (Zn₄(Si₂O₇)(OH)₂.H₂O); in small amounts in the oxidized zone of zinc deposits; associated with zincite and franklinite
Examples	major deposit at Franklin and Sterling Hill, New Jersey (USA); others at Moresnet and Vieille Montagne (Belgium), Greenland, South Africa, Zaire and Zambia

Olivine $(Mg,Fe)_2SiO_4$

Olivine is the name for a group of minerals. They vary from the magnesian olivine *forsterite* to the iron olivine *fayalite*. But the most common olivine is of intermediate composition and has a pleasant olive-green colour, from which its name is derived. Olivine is an important rock-forming mineral. It is an essential mineral in basic igneous rocks, such as olivine gabbro, and ultrabasic (silica-poor) rocks such as alkali olivine basalt and peridotite. Gem-quality specimens, called *peridot*, were used in the Middle Ages to decorate church robes and plates. They are now used in jewellery.

Olivine nodule

Olivine

garnet

olivine

mica

feldspar

Peridot

OLIVINE

*Colour	shades of green; forsterite, white or yellow; fayalite, brown or black
Lustre	vitreous
Transparency	transparent to translucent
Streak	colourless or white
Hardness	6.5 (fayalite)–7 (forsterite)
Cleavage	usually poorly developed
*Fracture	conchoidal; brittle
Habit	good crystals rare; usually isolated grains in igneous rocks, or granular masses
Twinning	uncommon
Specific gravity	3.2 (forsterite)–4.4 (fayalite)
Other tests	decomposed by hydrochloric acid
Crystal system	orthorhombic
Alteration	readily to serpentine; oxidized crystals may look reddish
Occurence	an important rock-forming mineral in basic and ultrabasic igneous rocks; fayalite occurs rarely in some quartz-bearing igneous rocks; forsterite in metamorphosed siliceous dolomite; olivine in some meteorites
Examples	peridot in Germany, on St. John's Island (Egypt) and in Myanmar; fayalite in rhyolites in the USA and in granite pegmatites in Ireland; forsterite on Skye (Scotland)

Garnet: Pyralspite Garnets

$(Mg, Fe, Mn)_3Al_2Si_3O_{12}$

Garnet is the name for a family of minerals. Chemically, they are divided into two groups: pyralspite garnets and ugrandite garnets. Pyralspite garnets are *pyrope* (magnesium and aluminium), *almandine* (iron and aluminium) and *spessartine* (manganese and aluminium). Garnets are used as gemstones in jewellery and are often given incorrect names, such as 'Cape ruby' or 'Arizona spinel'. The beautiful deep red pyrope is one of the most popular. Almandine, one of the most widespread varieties, often occurs as large, perfect crystals. Spessartine, one of the more precious gemstones, is popular for its yellowish-orange colour.

Almandine in schist

GARNET

Colour	variable; red to nearly black (pyrope), red-brown to black (almandine), dark-red to brownish red (spessartine)
Lustre	vitreous to resinous
Transparency	transparent to translucent
Streak	whitish
Hardness	6.5–7.5
Cleavage	absent
Fracture	subconchoidal or uneven
Habit	crystals common; dodecahedra or icositetrahedra
Specific gravity	3.7–4.3
Crystal system	cubic
Occurrence	pyrope in ultrabasic igneous rocks and in detrital deposits; almandine common in medium- and high-grade schists and gneisses derived from argillaceous rocks, in metamorphosed igneous rocks, and in heavy detrital residues in sediments; spessartine rarely in acid igneous rocks and in skarn deposits
Examples	pyrope in South Africa, Russia, the USA; gem almandine in Sri Lanka and India; spessartine in Sri Lanka, Madagascar, Myanmar, Brazil, Tanzania, Germany and Italy

Three faces of rombdodecahedron

Spessartine in marble

Garnet: Ugrandite Garnets
$Ca_3(Al,Cr,Fe)_2Si_3O_{12}$

The ugrandite garnets are *uvarovite* (calcium and chromium), *grossular* (calcium and aluminium) and *andradite* (calcium and iron). Most crystals are mixed, so that there is a partial replacement of some elements by others. The beautiful, deep emerald-green uvarovite is one of the rarest gemstones. Grossular gets its name from the botanical name for 'gooseberry', which it resembles in colour and shape. It is unusual among garnets in that it luminesces strongly in ultraviolet light. The green variety of andradite used as a gemstone is called *demantoid*, after the Old French word *diamant*, meaning diamond. Demantoid has a high dispersion comparable with diamond. Garnet is derived from the Latin *granatus* meaning 'like a grain'.

Grossular

GARNET

Colour	green (uvarovite); colourless to white, green, brown or pink (grossular); yellow, green, brown or black (andradite)
Lustre	vitreous to resinous
Transparency	translucent
Streak	whitish
Hardness	6.5–7.5
Cleavage	absent
Fracture	subconchoidal or uneven
Habit	crystals common; dodecahedra or icositetrahedra
Specific gravity	3.4–4.1 depending on composition
Crystal system	cubic
Occurrence	uvarovite is found in serpentinites rich in chromite; grossular occurs in marbles associated with calcite, diopside, wollastonite and vesuvianite; andradite is produced by contact metamorphism of limestones accompanied by the introduction of iron; also in syenite, serpentinite and chlorite schists
Examples	uvarovite in the former USSR, Finland, the USA, Canada; grossular crystals in Sri Lanka, Norway, Mexico; andradite in the former USSR, Italy, Tanzania and Zaire

Uvarovite

Andradite

Grossular

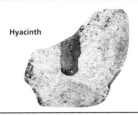

Tetragonal crystals

Hyacinth

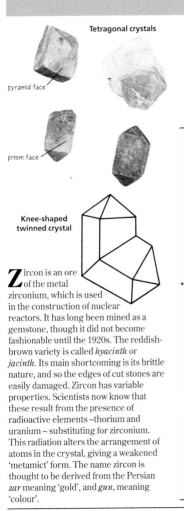

pyramid face

prism face

Knee-shaped twinned crystal

Zircon is an ore of the metal zirconium, which is used in the construction of nuclear reactors. It has long been mined as a gemstone, though it did not become fashionable until the 1920s. The reddish-brown variety is called *hyacinth* or *jacinth*. Its main shortcoming is its brittle nature, and so the edges of cut stones are easily damaged. Zircon has variable properties. Scientists now know that these result from the presence of radioactive elements –thorium and uranium – substituting for zirconium. This radiation alters the arrangement of atoms in the crystal, giving a weakened 'metamict' form. The name zircon is thought to be derived from the Persian *zar* meaning 'gold', and *gun*, meaning 'colour'.

ZIRCON

*Colour	usually light brown to red-brown; also yellowish, green, colourless, purplish
Lustre	vitreous to adamantine
Transparency	transparent to translucent, occasionally nearly opaque
Streak	colourless
*Hardness	7.5 (6.5 metamict form)
Cleavage	prismatic, indistinct
Fracture	conchoidal; very brittle
*Habit	prismatic crystals terminated by pyramids
Twinning	common, forming knee-shaped twins
*Specific gravity	4.6–4.7
Other tests	coloured varieties become colourless and transparent when heated
Crystal system	tetragonal
Occurrence	one of the commonest accessories of acid and intermediate igneous rocks; also in schists and gneisses; commonly occurs as rounded detrital grains in sands and sandstones
Examples	in alkaline rocks of the former USSR; in syenites and pegmatites in Norway; in gem gravels in Thailand; in beach sands in Australia; good crystals in Sri Lanka and in gold gravels in the former USSR; large crystals in Canada and the USA

Sillimanite Al_2SiO_5

Mineralogists describe sillimanite, kyanite and andalusite as *polymorphs* –that is, these minerals have the same chemical formula but different structures and properties. For example, they are stable under different temperatures, sillimanite being the high-temperature form. All three break down on heating to 1300°C (2372°F) to form a mineral called *mullite* and a siliceous glass. All three minerals are mined for conversion to mullite which is used in making refractory (heat-resistant) bricks and porcelain. Large prismatic crystals of sillimanite may stand out on weathered rock surfaces. Intergrowths of the fibrous form *fibrolite*, with quartz are easily seen on weathered surfaces as they are pure white. Large masses of almost pure sillimanite (85 per cent) have been mined in India. Gem-quality sillimanite is rare, but it is occasionally used in jewellery and the manufacture of carved figurines. The name is in honour of Benjamin Silliman, professor of chemistry in the nineteenth century.

Prismatic crystals

SILLIMANITE

Colour	greyish white, yellow, brown, greyish green
Lustre	vitreous to almost adamantine
Transparency	transparent to translucent
Streak	colourless
Hardness	6–7
Cleavage	good, parallel to side face
Fracture	uneven
*Habit	long slender prisms or in a felted mass of fibres called fibrolite
Specific gravity	3.2–3.3
Crystal system	orthorhombic
Occurrence	in regional metamorphic rocks formed from clays (i.e. rich in aluminium), also occasionally in the inner zone of hornfelses
Examples	blue, transparent sillimanite found at Mogok (Myanmar); greyish green varieties in gravels in Sri Lanka; water-worn masses in diamond-bearing sands at Minas Gerais (Brazil); massive fibrous sillimanite cobbles from Clearwater River valley, Idaho (USA); Maldan (Bohemia), Freiburg (Saxony)

Fibrolite

Prismatic crystals of andalusite

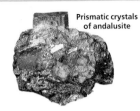

A ndalusite is the low-pressure, low-density form of the three aluminium silicate polymorphs (see sillimanite and kyanite). Petrologists find it a useful indicator of the conditions of metamorphism that existed when the rocks containing it were formed. Andalusite has been mined in large quantities in California and is used as a raw material for refractory (heat-resistant) linings. It is also used in high-temperature electrical insulators and in special acid-resistant porcelains. Transparent crystals may be used as gems. Well known examples are the rich green pebbles of andalusite found in Sri Lanka and Minas Gerais, Brazil. These crystals may show colour changes to reddish oranges owing to the property *pleochroism*, which is pronounced in andalusite. The large crystals found in Andalusia, Spain – from which the mineral is named – are mainly altered to white mica and quartz. Crystals up to 20 cm (8 in) long and 5 cm (2 in) thick occur at Lisenz, Austria. When broken across, the variety *chiastolite* shows a black cross, which is formed from carbonaceous impurities. Chiastolite is common in schists near Santiago de Compostela in Spain. It was once worn as an amulet.

ANDALUSITE

Colour	white, pink, pearl-grey, may be green or brown
Lustre	vitreous
Transparency	translucent to opaque
Streak	white
***Hardness**	7.5
Cleavage	prismatic, distinct
Fracture	uneven; tough, brittle
***Habit**	prismatic crystals of square cross-section, also granular or massive
Specific gravity	3.2
Crystal system	orthorhombic
Alteration	to a shimmer aggregate of white mica and quartz, which often coats the crystals
Occurrence	in clays which have been affected either by thermal metamorphism or by low pressure regional metamorphism; in pegmatites where it may be associated with corundum, tourmaline and topaz
Examples	crystals in Austria; in radial aggregates in pegmatites in the former Czechoslovakia; also in the former USSR, Brazil, Australia; chiastolite in England and the former USSR; large crosses from the former USSR

Chiastolite

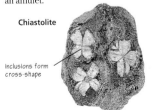

inclusions form cross-shape

Kyanite Al_2SiO_5

Kyanite is also known as disthene, meaning 'double strength'. This refers to the fact that the hardness along the length of kyanite crystals is less than the hardness across them. This is the mineral's most characteristic feature. Kyanite is mined in several parts of the world for use as a refractory material. Transparent crystals are occasionally used in jewellery. The most valued colours are deep cornflower-blue, pale azure-blue and bluish-green. Like the other aluminium silicate polymorphs, kyanite is an indicator of metamorphic conditions. It is formed at moderate temperatures and at moderate to high pressures in pelitic rocks, and is often associated with garnet, staurolite and corundum. The name is derived from the Greek word *kyanos*, meaning 'a dark blue substance'.

Bladed crystals

Kyanite

Kyanite

kyanite porphyroblasts

KYANITE

*Colour	blue, sometimes white or colourless at margins
Lustre	vitreous, pearly on cleavage surfaces
Transparency	transparent to subtranslucent
Streak	white
*Hardness	5–7 varying with direction
*Cleavage	two good cleavages
Fracture	brittle
*Habit	as flat, bladed crystals in schists and gneisses, and as radiating rosettes in quartz
Specific gravity	3.5–3.7
Twinning	frequent
Crystal system	triclinic
Alteration	to a shimmer aggregate of white mica and quartz
Occurrence	in regionally metamorphosed rocks, i.e. schists, gneisses, eclogites and amphibolites; may be associated with garnet or staurolite; also in associated pegmatites and quartz veins; a detrital mineral
Examples	good blue crystals at Pizzo Forno (Switzerland), enormous crystals in Brazil; green crystals up to 30 cm (12 in) long in Kenya; large deposit in the USA; also India, Kenya and Australia

$Al_2SiO_4(OH,F)_2$ **Topaz**

People have valued topaz as a gemstone since the times of ancient Greece. Its qualities are its hardness, pleasant colour and high lustre. It occurs in a variety of delicate colours, the most prized being pink, blue and honey-yellow. Some stones change colour on heating. For example, yellow topaz from Brazil turns red if heated to 300°–450°C (572°–842°F) and cooled slowly to prevent cracking. Topaz crystals weigh up to 300 kg (661 lb). The largest cut topaz, a pale blue Brazilian Princess, was found at Teófilo Otoni, north of Rio de Janeiro. It weighed 4265.5 g (21,327 carats or 150 oz).

Massive white topaz

Yellow topaz crystal

striated prism faces

Topaz and quartz on orthoclase

quartz   orthoclase

TOPAZ

Colour	colourless, straw-yellow, pale blue or green
Lustre	vitreous
Transparency	transparent to sub-translucent
Streak	colourless
***Hardness**	8
***Cleavage**	basal, perfect
Fracture	sub-conchoidal to uneven
***Habit**	prismatic crystals, vertically striated; also columnar or granular
***Specific gravity**	3.4–3.6
Other tests	sometimes fluorescent in yellow, cream or pale green
Crystal system	orthorhombic
Occurrence	a pneumatolytic mineral, in granite and pegmatites, associated with tourmaline, cassiterite and fluorspar; also as round translucent pebbles in alluvium as a secondary deposit
Examples	the largest crystals come from Brazil and Siberia; azure-blue topazes from the former USSR; placer deposits from the River Sanarka (Urals), Sri Lanka and Mexico; good crystals from Japan; major localities in the USA are Colorado, Utah and California

Staurolite $(Fe,Mg)_2(Al,Fe)_9(Si_4O_{20})(O,OH)_2$

The term staurolite comes from the Greek word *stauros* meaning 'cross', because the mineral is famous for its cross-, plus- or X-shaped interpenetrant twinned crystals. Cross- or plus-shaped twins are known as 'fairy stones' in North Carolina, USA, and are sold as amulets, although many of these are dyed imitations made from rock. Plus-shaped twins and dark brown, transparent crystals are sometimes used as gemstones. Staurolite occurs as large crystals (*porphyroblasts*) in schists and gneisses formed from argillaceous sediments in which sufficient iron is present. It is commonly associated with kyanite, garnet, tourmaline and sillimanite. It stands out as yellowish brown prisms on weathered rocks.

Interpenetrant twin

STAUROLITE

*Colour	reddish brown, also brownish black yellowish brown; grey when altered
Lustre	vitreous to resinous
Transparency	usually translucent to opaque, rarely transparent
Streak	colourless when fresh
Hardness	7–7.5
Cleavage	fair, in one direction
Fracture	conchoidal to uneven
Habit	usually in well-developed prismatic crystals
*Twinning	famous for interpenetrant twins, to give cross-, plus-, or X-shaped twins; rarely massive
Specific gravity	3.4–3.8
Other tests	infusible, insoluble in acids
Crystal system	monoclinic
Alteration	surfaces often have an earthy coating due to alteration
Occurrence	a metamorphic mineral typical of medium temperature regional metamorphism; may occur with kyanite (often as parallel intergrowths), also garnet, tourmaline and sillimanite; also as a detrital mineral in alluvial sands
Examples	large crystals in Moravia, Bavaria and Scotland; cruciform twins in the USA and France; in mica schists in Switzerland

staurolite porphyroblasts **Staurolite schist**

staurolite porphyroblasts

Staurolite schist

The name sphene comes from the Greek word *sphen*, meaning 'wedge', because the crystals are commonly wedge-shaped. The mineral is not widely used in jewellery, because the clear green, yellow or brownish stones used as gems are rare. These crystals are brilliant, but they are comparatively soft. Other varieties of sphene may be opaque. Sphene is a source of titanium oxide, which is used as a pigment in paint. Sphene is widely distributed as an accessory mineral in igneous rocks. It also occurs in metamorphic schists, gneisses and marbles. The most economically important occurrence of sphene is in the Kola Peninsula, the former USSR. The alternative name titanite refers to the high titanium content. The element titanium was named after the Titans, the mythical sons of the Earth.

Massive form

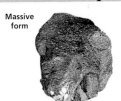

SPHENE

Colour	yellow, green, brown, reddish brown, red or black
Lustre	vitreous, inclining to adamantine
Transparency	transparent to opaque
Streak	white
Hardness	5–5.5
Cleavage	moderate, prismatic
Fracture	conchoidal; brittle
Habit	disseminated crystals, usually wedge- or envelope-shaped; occurs also in compact or lamellar masses and in disseminated grains
Twinning	common, giving sharp re-entrant angles
Specific gravity	3.4–3.6
Other tests	fuses with swelling on the edges to a dark-coloured glass; partly decomposed by hydrochloric acid, completely by sulphuric acid
Crystal system	monoclinic
Alteration	to rutile, ilmenite and others
Occurrence	an important accessory of many igneous rocks, e.g. hornblende granite, syenite and diorite; also in schists and lime-rich rocks altered by contact metamorphism
Examples	classic localities in the Alps; large crystals in Bridgewater, Bucks County, USA; gem-quality in Mexico

Massive form

Crystals

1942

Idocrase $Ca_{10}(Mg,Fe)_2Al_4Si_9O_{34}(OH,F)_4$

Massive forms of idocrase are often mistaken for diopside, epidote or garnet, while crystals resemble minerals of similar colour, such as diopside, green garnet, olivine and tourmaline. Idocrase is essentially a mineral of contact metamorphism. Its high calcium content reflects its occurrence in limestones. It is also called *vesuvianite* after a green variety found in blocks of dolomitic limestone erupted from Mount Vesuvius, Italy. Gem quality crystals are rare, but are extracted for cutting at Litchfield in Pontiac County and Templeton in Ottowa County, Quebec, Canada. Most idocrase used in jewellery is in smoothly polished, rounded shapes. A green, massive variety of idocrase – *californite* – is used as a jade substitute, called *Vesuvian Jade* in the trade. Other forms are a blue variety, *cyprine*, found at Arendal, Norway, and a pale-green, boron-containing variety, *wiluite*, found in Siberia. Transparent crystals are rare. Larger specimens are used for small receptacles and figurines. The name is from the Greek *eidos* meaning 'likeness' and *krasis* meaning 'mixture', alluding to its similarity to other minerals.

Pale brown striated crystals

striations parallel to length

Dark green prismatic crystals

IDOCRASE

Colour	brown to yellow-brown or green; blue form called cyprine
Lustre	vitreous to resinous
Transparency	transparent to translucent
Streak	white
Hardness	6–7
Cleavage	poor
Fracture	uneven; brittle
*Habit	prismatic crystals often striated lengthwise; also massive, granular or columnar
Specific gravity	3.3–3.4
Crystal system	tetragonal
Occurrence	in contact metamorphosed impure limestones along with grossular garnet, diopside, wollastonite, epidote and calcite
Examples	Zermatt (Swiss Alps), Mount Vesuvius, Monzoni, Piedmont (Italy), Gopfergrun, Fichtelgebirge (Germany), Ciclova (Romania), Arendal (Norway), the Urals (the former USSR), Litchfield, Quebec and Templeton, Ontario (Canada), Magnet Cove, Arkansas and Sanford, Maine (USA)

Dioptase is a relatively rare emerald-green mineral, sometimes tinged bluish or blackish. It has no industrial importance, but is popular with collectors. It has been called 'copper emerald' or 'the emerald of the poor'. Dioptase crystals mined at Mount Altyn-Tyube, USSR, were first thought to be emeralds. But their low hardness easily distinguishes them from emeralds – one reason why dioptase is not more valued. The crystals found in Zaire, at Reneville, are quite large and may be cut for jewellery. Dioptase has only had general recognition in Europe since it was introduced in 1780 to St. Petersburg, where it was wrongly identified as a variety of emerald called *achrite*. A related copper silicate mineral is *Chrysocolla* ((Cu,A1) $SiO_3.H_2O$), which is probably amorphous. It forms green to blue-green encrustations and fillings of enamel-like or earthy texture. Fine cleavages in dioptase crystals sometimes give a pearly lustre and interesting internal reflections. This accounts for its name which comes from Greek words for 'through' and 'visible'.

Crystals

Crystals

DIOPTASE

*Colour	emerald-green
Lustre	vitreous
Transparency	transparent to translucent
Streak	green
*Hardness	5
Cleavage	rhombohedral, perfect
Fracture	conchoidal to uneven, brittle
Habit	short, prismatic crystals often terminated by rhombohedra; massive
Specific gravity	3.3
Crystal system	trigonal
Occurrence	uncommon; found in the weathered zones of copper sulphide deposits
Examples	Kazakhstan (the former USSR), Reneville (Zaire), minor deposits at Baita (Romania), Copiapo (Chile), Mammoth Mine, Tiger, Arizona (USA) and Otavi Range at Guchabo (Namibia)

Epidote $Ca_2(Al,Fe)_3Si_3O_{12}(OH)$

Epidote forms a continuous series of minerals, ending with clinozoisite, which contains no iron. Epidote has a characteristic yellow-green colour. It may be mistaken for tourmaline, which lacks cleavage and has a triangular or hexagonal cross-section. *Withamite* is a pink, manganese-bearing epidote found in vesicles and veins in andesite. *Pumpellyite*, a widely distributed, hydrous epidote-like mineral, is found in low-grade metamorphic rocks, and also in the vesicles of ancient lavas. *Pistacite* is a pistachio-green variety. Epidote is a widespread mineral. It is common in medium- or low-grade metamorphic rocks which have formed either from calcareous or basic rocks. It occurs in 'saussurite', the alteration product of plagioclase feldspar, and is formed from the alteration of hornblende.

Prismatic crystals of epidote

striations parallel to length

EPIDOTE

*Colour	yellowish green to greenish black (epidote); greenish grey (clinozoisite)
Lustre	vitreous
Transparency	transparent to nearly opaque
Streak	white or grey–brown
Hardness	6–7
Cleavage	one perfect basal cleavage parallel to length of crystals
Fracture	uneven; brittle
*Habit	crystals elongated and often striated parallel to length; also massive, fibrous, or granular
Twinning	uncommon
Specific gravity	3.2–3.5 (increasing with iron-content)
Other tests	epidote fuses with swelling to a black magnetic glass
Crystal system	monoclinic
Occurrence	found in medium- to low-grade metamorphic rocks; epidote associated with garnet, diopside, idocrase and calcite in impure limestones in contact aureoles; formed by hydrothermal alteration of plagioclase in gabbros; in vesicles in basic lava flows
Examples	good crystals in Austria, Norway, France; pink crystals in Italy; in metabasites in Cyprus

Withamite

Massive epidote

Z oisite is a member of the epidote group of minerals, although it belongs to the orthorhombic rather than the monoclinic crystal system. *Thulite*, a pink, manganese-bearing variety from Norway, has been used in jewellery – *Thule* is an ancient Greek term for far northern countries. Transparent, bluish-violet crystals of another variety, called *tanzanite*, have been called the 'blue treasure of Africa'. They were first discovered near Arusha, Tanzania, in 1967, and the largest specimen found to date weighed 126 carats (25 g). Tanzanite can be created artificially by heating green zoisite to a temperature of 380° C (716° F), at which it turns blue-violet. Zoisite is similar in appearance and occurrence to clinozoisite, but is less common.

Thulite

Uncut tanzanite

Cut tanzanite

Chrome zoisite
with ruby

ZOISITE

*Colour	grey to white, pale green or yellow-brown; thulite, rose-pink
Lustre	vitreous, pearly on cleavage surfaces
Transparency	transparent to translucent
Streak	white
Hardness	6–6.5
Cleavage	one perfect cleavage
Fracture	uneven
Habit	prismatic crystals, often striated parallel to length; also massive, coarse- to fine-bladed or fibrous aggregates
Specific gravity	3.2–3.4
Crystal system	orthorhombic
Occurrence	forms like epidote and clinozoisite as a constituent of saussurite, resulting from the alteration of calcic plagioclases in gabbros; in metamorphic rocks, especially formed either from igneous rocks rich in calcic feldspars, or impure limestones; in metasomatic rocks may be associated with garnet, idocrase and actinolite
Examples	Austria, USA and former USSR; tanzanite from Tanzania; thulite in Norway, USA and Austria

Beryl $Be_3Al_2Si_6O_{18}$

Beryl is one of the oldest known minerals. The most prized variety *emerald* sometimes fetches higher prices than diamond. Emerald was mined in Upper Egypt in about 2000 BC. Queen Cleopatra is supposed to have owned an emerald on which her portrait was engraved. The short-sighted Roman emperor Nero may have used an emerald as a monocle, but historians now think that it was probably made of the pale blue variety *aquamarine*. Most blue aquamarines used in jewellery were originally greenish-yellow. The colour changes when they are heated to 400°–450°C (752°–842°F) and then cooled. Some beryl crystals are enormous. One discovered in Albany, Maine, was 6 m (20 ft) long.

Aquamarine

BERYL

*Colour	pale green to bright green (emerald), bluish-green (aquamarine), yellow and white
Lustre	vitreous
Transparency	transparent to translucent, opaque when full of inclusions
Streak	white
*Hardness	7.5–8
Cleavage	indistinct, basal
Fracture	conchoidal to uneven; brittle
Habit	simple hexagonal prisms, often striated vertically; also columnar, granular, and compact masses and in rounded grains
Specific gravity	2.6–2.8
*Crystal system	hexagonal
Alteration	alters to mica and kaolin
Occurrence	commonly found as an accessory mineral in acid igneous rocks, such as granite and pegmatite; also in gneiss, schist and slate, in limestone or in secondary deposits
Examples	aquamarines from Brazil, Nerchinsk Mountains, Transbaikalia and the Urals (the former USSR); emeralds from near Bogotá (Colombia), and Sverdlovsk (the former USSR); beryl is found in the Mourne Mountain granite (Ireland)

Pale green beryl

Beryl in feldspar

Emerald

The Vikings probably used bluish-white specimens of cordierite as navigational aids. They could tell the points of the compass even when the sky was overcast, because, depending on which way it was viewed, the mineral changed colour in polarized light. This distinctive feature is called *pleochroism*. The variety of cordierite, *dichroite*, may appear yellow or deep blue according to the way in which it is viewed, while the violet-coloured variety is called *iolite*. Although gem-quality cordierite is attractive and readily available it is not considered valuable and is not widely used. The best gemstones come from Madagascar and a pale form called *water sapphire* occurs in Sri Lanka. The iron-rich form is called *sekaninaite.* Granular cordierite resembles quartz, from which it is distinguished with difficulty. Unlike quartz, however, it can be found enwrapping other crystals. Cordiereite is named after P.L.A. Cordier who described it in detail.

Massive form

vitreous lustre

CORDIERITE

*Colour	smoky blue and violet; also grey, colourless, green or yellow; pleochroism visible to the naked eye
Lustre	vitreous to greasy
Transparency	transparent to translucent
Streak	white
Hardness	7
Cleavage	poor in one direction
Fracture	conchoidal to uneven; brittle
Habit	pseudo-hexagonal, short prismatic crystals; often as irregular and rounded grains, looking like quartz
Twinning	pseudo-hexagonal twins
Specific gravity	2.6–2.8
Crystal system	orthorhombic
Alteration	alters readily to mica, chlorite and talc
Occurrence	widespread in hornfels produced from argillaceous rocks, as oval bluish spots or cavities; also in gneisses and schists where pressure was low; may be found in norite or granite, where clay has been incorporated; associated with garnet, mica, quartz, andalusite, sillimanite, staurolite, chalcopyrite and spinel
Examples	Scotland, Sweden, Canada, USA; blue crystals from Sri Lanka used as gemstones (*saphir d'eau*)

Cordierite in gneiss

Tourmaline

$Na(Mg,Fe,Li,Al,Mn)_3Al_6(BO_3)_3O_{18}(OH,F)_4$

Tourmaline can show a variety of colours, even in a single crystal. The layers of the crystal may be arranged concentrically, parallel to the vertical axis of the crystal, or in longitudinal bands. Such tourmalines are called *moorheads*, or *turkheads* where the last colour is red. Some crystals are strongly pleochroic to the naked eye and are used as gemstones. Others change colour when moved from natural to artificial light. Red tourmaline, introduced to Europe from Sri Lanka in 1703, was found to have the special property of attracting tiny ash particles on heating. These were the first observations of pyroelectricity.

Tourmaline crystals in quartz and apatite

Green crystals

Rubellite

Elongate crystals in quartz

TOURMALINE

*Colour	usually pitch black or brown, also grey, yellow, green or red, and more rarely colourless or white; colours commonly zoned
Lustre	vitreous to resinous
Transparency	transparent to opaque
Streak	white
Hardness	7–7.5
Cleavage	not well marked
Fracture	conchoidal to uneven; brittle
*Habit	long prismatic crystals of curved triangular cross-section, vertically striated; the two ends of the crystal are often terminated differently; also columnar masses and radiating groups
Specific gravity	2.9–3.2
Other tests	strongly piezoelectric and pyroelectric
Crystal system	trigonal
Alteration	to muscovite, biotite or chlorite
Occurrence	a characteristic mineral of pegmatite dykes in granite, and in schorl formed by pneumatolytic alteration; also common in gneisses, schists and in crystalline limestones and dolomites; a heavy residue in many sedimentary rocks
Examples	crystals in Italy, Myanmar, Switzerland, Brazil, USA

(Mg,Fe)SiO₃ **Orthopyroxenes**

Pyroxenes are a widespread group of rock-forming silicates. The two main groups are orthopyroxenes and clinopyroxenes. The orthopyroxenes form a chemical series of which the most common are the magnesium-rich *enstatite* (Mg_2SiO_3) and the iron-containing *bronzite* and *hypersthene*. Hypersthene contains up to a 1:1 ratio of magnesium and iron, while bronzite is intermediate between enstatite and hypersthene. Pyroxenes are distinguished from another group of rock-forming silicates called amphiboles by having two cleavages, approximately at right angles to each other. The colour deepens with increasing iron content. Enstatite is usually light green, while hypersthene is a dark, brownish green.

Bronzite can be recognised by its characteristic bronze lustre.

Bronzite

Hypersthene

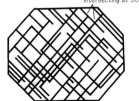

Orthopyroxenes

two cleavages, intersecting at 90°

ORTHOPYROXENES

*Colour	pale green to dark brownish green or black; bronze lustre for bronzite
Lustre	vitreous
Transparency	translucent to opaque
Hardness	5–6
*Cleavage	prismatic, good cleavages intersect close to right-angles
Fracture	uneven
Habit	stubby prismatic crystals; most often as grains, massive
Specific gravity	3.2–4 (iron-rich pyroxenes are more dense)
Crystal system	orthorhombic
Alteration	to serpentine minerals or fibrous amphibole
Occurrence	mostly as common constituents of basic and ultrabasic igneous rocks especially easily seen in gabbros and pyroxenites; in some andesites and stony meteorites; in some thermally metamorphosed shales and high-grade regionally metamorphosed rocks
Examples	California (USA), Donegal (Ireland), Cima de Gagnone (Switzerland), Troodos (Cyprus) and New York (USA); bronzite in Transvaal (South Africa) and Montana (USA)

Clinopyroxenes $Ca(Mg,Fe)Al,Fe,Ti(Si,Al)_2O_6$

Clinopyroxenes are abundant rock-forming minerals. They vary in composition more than orthopyroxenes. *Augite* and *pigeonite* are calcium-poor varieties found in basalts, dolerites and andesites. *Diopside* and *hedenbergite* occur in metamorphic rocks. *Titanaugite*, found in alkali-gabbros and alkali olivine basalts, has a high titanium content and is violet or purple-brown. *Omphacite* is an unusually bright green mineral found in eclogites. Other clinopyroxenes are the sodium-containing *aegerine* ($NaFeSi_2O_6$), *spodumene* ($LiAlSi_2O_6$), an ore of lithium, and *jadeite* ($NaAlSi_2O_6$), which is used as the ornamental stone jade.

Aegerine

CLINOPYROXENES

Colour dark green to black (augite)

Lustre vitreous

Transparency translucent to opaque

Hardness 5.5–6.5

Cleavage prismatic good, sometimes basal parting present

Fracture uneven

Habit stubby crystals of square or eight-sided cross-section; granular, massive

Twinning common

Specific gravity 3.2–3.6

Crystal system monoclinic

Occurrence augite is common in such igneous rocks as gabbros, basalts, pyroxenites and diorites; also in some high-grade metamorphic rocks; diopside and hedenbergite occur in a number of metamorphic rocks, diopside in metamorphosed impure limestones, hedenbergite in metamorphosed iron-rich sediments

Examples augite in South Africa, Greenland and USA; hedenbergite in Italy, Norway and Japan; diopside in Switzerland, Vesuvius (Italy), the Zillertal (Austria) and the Urals and Lake Baikal (the former USSR)

Hedenbergite

Spodumene

Augite crystals

short prismatic crystals

surface alteration to
black manganese oxide

**Granular
rhodonite**

Wollastonite

**Polished
rhodonite**

WOLLASTONITE

*Colour	white or greyish
Lustre	vitreous
Transparency	subtransparent to translucent
Hardness	4.5–5
*Cleavage	one perfect, two good
Fracture	uneven
Habit	crystals tabular or short prisms; massive, compact or fibrous
Twinning	common
Specific gravity	2.8–3.1
*Other tests	dissolves in hydrochloric acid depositing silica
Crystal system	triclinic
*Occurrence	in thermally metamorphosed limestones at igneous contacts, often associated with calcium-rich garnets and diopside; the silica may have been introduced from the igneous rocks
Examples	wollastonite in the Black Forest (Germany), Brittany (France), Csiklowa (Romania), Crestmore, California (USA) and Pargos (Finland); rhodonite at Broken Hill, NSW (Australia), Sverdlovsk, the Urals (the former USSR) and Langban (Sweden)

Wollastonite, which was once called *tabular spar*, occurs in impure limestones that have been altered by heat. It often occurs in association with tremolite, from which it can be distinguished by its solubility in hydrochloric acid. Wollastonite is used in refractories and some paints. A related mineral, *rhodonite*, whose formula is $((Mn,Fe,Ca)SiO_3)$, is associated with manganese ore deposits in hydrothermal veins or found in metamorphosed manganese-bearing sediments. Rhodonite is a pink to brown mineral that weathers to black, and is used as a decorative stone. Wollastonite and rhodonite belong to the pyroxenoid group, which are related to the pyroxenes. Wollastonite is named after W.H. Wollaston, the British mineralogist.

Anthophyllite $(Mg,Fe)_7Si_8O_{22}(OH)_2$

Anthophyllite belongs to the amphibole group – an important group of rock-forming silicates in igneous and metamorphic rocks. Amphiboles are hydrous minerals and they break down by losing water during high-temperature metamorphism. Also belonging to the amphibole group is the mineral cummingtonite $((Mg,Fe)_7Si_8O_{22}(OH)_2)$. Though not forming a distinct chemical series, anthophyllite and cummingtonite are so alike that mineralogists can identify them only by detailed optical or X-ray tests. Cummingtonite forms a chemical series with *grunerite*, which is the iron-rich member. The aluminium-rich variety of anthophyllite is called *gedrite*. Asbestos-grade anthophyllite is called *amosite*.

Anthophyllite

Cummingtonite

Aggregate of fibrous anthophyllite

ANTHOPHYLLITE

*Colour	white, grey, green, brown (anthophyllite) brown (cummingtonite)
Lustre	vitreous, silky when fibrous
Transparency	translucent
Hardness	5–6
Cleavage	prismatic, perfect
Fracture	uneven
Habit	usually fibrous aggregates; crystals rare
Twinning	common in cummingtonite
Specific gravity	2.8–3.4 (anthophyllite); 3.2–3.6 (cummingtonite)
Crystal system	orthorhombic (anthophyllite); monoclinic (cummingtonite)
Occurrence	anthophyllite is a metamorphic mineral of magnesium-rich sediments associated with cordierite; cummingtonite is a metamorphic mineral of regionally metamorphosed basic igneous rocks and some hornfelses
Examples	anthophyllite at Kongsberg (Norway), Fahlan (Sweden), Orijarvi (Finland); cummingtonite at Cummington, Massachusetts (USA) and Orijarvi (Finland); grunerite in the iron deposits of Lake Superior (USA)

$Ca_2(Mg,Fe)_5Si_8O_{22}(OH,F)_2$ **Tremolite-Actinolite**

Tremolite and actinolite are amphiboles that form a chemical series. Tremolite contains little or no iron and is almost colourless. The iron content in actinolite produces a green colour, the most attractive variety being *nephrite*, or *greenstone*, the more common form of jade. Nephrite is tough and takes a good polish. Beautiful nephrites in New Zealand are called Maori stone, because of their widespread use in ancient Maori art. Tremolite and actinolite often occur in fibrous masses. They were the first such materials to be called asbestos. Fibrous tremolite is used for insulating and fire-proofing. They both occur in relatively low-grade metamorphic rocks. Actinolite is characteristic of the greenschist facies. Tremolite was discovered in Tremola, a valley in the Alps.

Actinolite

TREMOLITE-ACTINOLITE

*Colour	white or grey (tremolite) to dark green (actinolite)
Lustre	vitreous, silky when fibrous
Transparency	transparent to translucent
Hardness	5–6
Cleavage	prismatic, good, (120° cleavage angle)
Fracture	uneven
*Habit	long bladed or prismatic crystals; massive or fibrous
Twinning	common
Specific gravity	3–3.4
Crystal system	monoclinic
Alteration	to talc (tremolite); to chlorite, epidote, serpentine and calcite (actinolite)
Occurrence	characteristic of thermally metamorphosed magnesian limestones associated with dolomite, calcite, diopside, forsterite and quartz; in altered ultrabasic rocks associated with talc; actinolite occurs in some schists associated with albite, chlorite and epidote, especially metabasic rocks
Examples	tremolite in Switzerland, New York (USA) and the Urals (the former USSR); actinolite in Austria and Italy; nephrite in central Asia

Tremolite

Nephrite

Asbestos

Hornblende $(Ca,Na)_{2-3}(Mg,Fe,Al)_5(Si,Al)_8O_{22}(OH)_2$

Hornblende

Hornblende is an amphibole whose composition varies widely. This gives rise to a number of varieties. *Edenite* is a pale green hornblende, poor in iron, while *pargasite* is a dark green or bluish green type, rich in iron. *Basaltic hornblende*, which occurs in iron-rich basic igneous rocks, contains titanium and sodium and is brown or black. Like other amphiboles, hornblende is distinguished from pyroxenes, which are often similar in appearance, by having two cleavages at an angle of 120°. Hornblende is a widespread and abundant rock-forming mineral. It is characteristic of medium-grade metabasic rocks known as amphibolites. It is a common consitutent of syenites and diorites. The name is derived from the German words meaning 'horn' and 'to blind', in reference to its lustre.

Hornblende

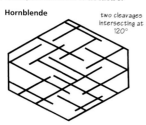

two cleavages intersecting at 120°

Hornblende with red garnet

HORNBLENDE

*Colour	light green to dark green (almost black)
Lustre	vitreous
Transparency	translucent to nearly opaque
Streak	white to grey
Hardness	5–6
*Cleavage	prismatic, good (120° cleavage angle)
Fracture	uneven
Habit	long or short prismatic crystals, massive, granular or fibrous
Twinning	common
Specific gravity	3–3.5
Crystal system	monoclinic
Occurrence	very widespread in igneous rocks especially intermediate and acid types; major mineral in metamorphosed basic rocks; uncommon in metamorphosed dolomites and ironstones
Examples	Edenville, New York (USA), Pargas and Pernio (Finland), Hurry Inlet (Greenland) and Ontario (Canada)

Glaucophane-Riebeckite

$$Na_2(Mg,Fe,Al)_5Si_8O_{22}(OH)_2$$

The glaucophane-riebeckite series of amphiboles have characteristic colours, the deeper shades of riebeckite reflecting its higher iron content. Fibrous riebeckite, called *crocidolite* or *blue asbestos*, has been mined in South Africa and elsewhere for insulating material. It is now regarded as harmful, crocidolite being a greater health hazard than crystotile asbestos. A related blue-green mineral *arfvedsonite* is found in highly alkaline syenites and associated pegmatites. *Tiger's eye* is a silicified form of crocidolite which has been weathered to yellow and brown. Glaucophane is the essential amphibole in blueschists, which are metamorphosed sediments formed at high pressure and low temperature. Riebeckite occurs in alkaline igneous rocks, particularly alkali granites.

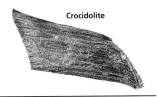
Crocidolite

Glaucophane

Riebeckite

GLAUCOPHANE- RIEBECKITE

*Colour	grey, grey-blue or lavender blue (glaucophane); dark blue or black (riebeckite)
Lustre	vitreous, silky when fibrous
Transparency	translucent
Streak	white to light blue
Hardness	5–6
Cleavage	prismatic, good
Fracture	uneven
Habit	prismatic or acicular crystals, rare; common as fibrous aggregates
Twinning	common
Specific gravity	3–3.4
Crystal system	monoclinic
Occurrence	glaucophane is a metamorphic mineral found in schists derived from greywackes and clays via low-temperature, high-pressure metamorphism; riebeckite in soda trachytes, rhyolites and granites
Examples	glaucophane as crystals in schists at Piedmont (Italy); as fibrous aggregates in California (USA), Groix Island (France), Svalbard (Norway) and western Alps; riebeckite as crystals in granite at Quincy, Massachusetts (USA) and in schists in Galicia (Spain); crocidolite in South Africa, Australia and Brazil

Muscovite $KAl_2(AlSi_3O_{10})(OH,F)_2$

Muscovite is a widespread member of the mica group of minerals. It is best known as a mostly colourless, flaky mineral which can form enormous crystals, up to 9–15 m² (100–160 sq ft), in some pegmatites. The first window panes were made of muscovite and it is still used in oil stoves and lamps, because it resists heat. Varieties include *sericite*, a fine-grained white mica, *illite*, a degraded white mica found in soils, *paragonite*, a sodium-containing variety found rarely in some schists, and *glauconite*, a green mineral which is found in greensands. An allied lithium-containing mineral *lepidolite* is an attractive pink.

basal cleavage surface

Muscovite

Mica pegmatite

books of mica

Muscovite

Crystals

cleavage

MUSCOVITE

*Colour	colourless or pale grey, green or brown
Lustre	vitreous, pearly parallel to cleavage
Transparency	transparent to translucent
*Hardness	2–2.5
*Cleavage	basal, perfect; cleavage flakes flexible and elastic
Habit	crystals tabular and hexagonal in outline; foliated masses or 'books'; small scales and plates
Twinning	common
Specific gravity	2.8–2.9
Crystal system	monoclinic (pseudo-hexagonal)
Alteration	very resistant to weathering
Occurrence	widespread in low temperature granites alongside biotite; in greisens and especially in pegmatites as large crystals; abundant in schists and gneisses; it is a common detrital mineral resistant to weathering and easily moved by water due to its lightness and flaky form
Examples	in pegmatites in Ontario (Canada), New Hampshire and South Dakota (USA), throughout the Alps, Bihar and Madras (India) and in Brazil

112

$K(Mg,Fe)_3AlSi_3O_{10}(OH,F)_2$ **Biotite-Phlogopite**

These micas form a series ranging from dark, iron-rich biotites to the pale phlogopite $(KMg_3AlSi_3O_{10}(OH,F)_2)$. Phlogopite has a higher resistance to heat than muscovite and has similar uses. Like muscovite, these micas can occur as huge crystals up to 2 m (6.6 ft) in diameter. Biotite often forms the dark mineral in granites. Its crystal form as small scales and plates distinguishes it from hornblende. The alignment of biotite crystals, alongside those of chlorite and muscovite, often gives metamorphic rocks their characteristic fabric.

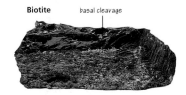

Biotite basal cleavage

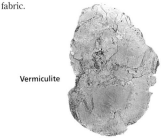

Vermiculite

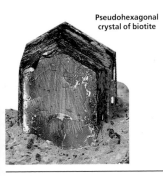

Pseudohexagonal crystal of biotite

BIOTITE-PHLOGOPITE

*Colour	phlogopite is golden brown; biotite is dark green-brown or black
Lustre	vitreous or pearly in phlogopite, submetallic, splendent in biotite
Transparency	transparent to translucent
*Hardness	2.5–3
*Cleavage	basal, perfect
Habit	tabular, pseudo-hexagonal crystals, lamellar aggregates or disseminated flakes
Twinning	common
Specific gravity	2.7–3.3 (increasing with iron content)
Crystal system	monoclinic (pseudo-hexagonal)
Occurrence	phlogopite in marbles produced by metamorphism of siliceous dolomitic limestones; magnesium-rich biotites in mica-periodotites and kimberlite; biotite widespread in granite, syenite and diorite and fine-grained equivalents; biotite occurs in many schists and gneisses
Examples	large biotites in pegmatites in the Ilmen Mountains (the former USSR), Greenland, Scandinavia and Brazil; phlogopite in Switzerland, Finland, Canada and Sri Lanka

Chlorite $(Mg,Fe,Al)_6(Si,Al)_4O_{10}(OH)_8$

Chlorite is the name of a group of minerals related to the micas, but which do not contain any sodium or potassium. One variety *clinochore* occurs as monoclinic tabular crystals. *Penninite* occurs as pseudo-hexagonal crystals which can be very large. Fine examples occur in Zermatt, Switzerland, and Zillertal, Austria. The variety *ripidolite* usually occurs in scaly masses or in radiating or tubular form. Chlorite is an abundant mineral in many low-grade metamorphic rocks, such as chlorite-schists and chlorite-phyllites. In low- to medium-grade, regionally metamorphosed rocks, chlorite may be associated with the mineral chloritoid. The latter bears a superficial resemblance to chlorite, from which it is named, but differs in composition. Chlorite may be distinguished from chloritoid by its flexible, but inelastic flakes (flakes of chloritoid are brittle) and a much lower hardness (2–2.5 against 6.5). Because chlorite has a varied chemical composition and is stable at low-temperatures it occurs in a wide variety of rock types formed at low temperatures. The name chlorite comes from the Greek *khloros*, which means 'yellow-green'. This describes the mineral's typical colour.

Ripidolite

Chlorite

CHLORITE

*Colour	mainly pale or bright green
Lustre	pearly
Transparency	translucent to opaque
*Hardness	2–2.5
*Cleavage	perfect basal, giving flexible flakes
Habit	six-sided tabular crystals; foliated masses or scales, often radiating fan-shapes
Twinning	common
Specific gravity	2.6–3.3
Other tests	greasy feel when in flakes
Crystal system	monoclinic
Occurrence	widespread as late-stage mineral or secondary product in vesicles and veins in igneous rocks; alteration product of ferromagnesian minerals and volcanic glasses; weathering and diagenetic product in sediments, especially greywackes; in low-grade phyllites and schists
Examples	Amity, New York (USA), the Urals (the former USSR), Zermatt (Switzerland), Bavaria (Germany) and Zillertal (Austria)

Green serpentine

Yellow serpentine

fibrous serpentine

Serpentine is the name for a group of common secondary minerals. The group includes *chrysotile*, a type of asbestos that forms fibrous yellow-white or green aggregates with a silky lustre, *lizardite*, a compact, whitish variety made up of tiny plates, and *antigorite*, which is lamellar and occurs as tough, compact, dark green masses. Serpentine minerals are formed by low-temperature hydration of ultramafic rocks, including dunite and pyroxenite. Coloured varieties are used for ornaments and internal decorations, because their low hardness makes them easy to work. The name serpentine refers to the snake-like appearance of the massive form.

Chrysotile

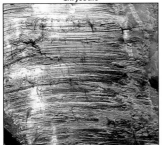

SERPENTINE

*Colour	pale to dark green, may be stained dull red
*Lustre	silky to waxy or dull
Transparency	opaque, occasionally translucent
Hardness	2.5–3.5
Cleavage	perfect basal in flaky varieties
Fracture	conchoidal or splintery
Habit	chrysotile forms small veins with fibres at right angles to the walls; lizardite is compact; antigorite in flakes
Specific gravity	2.5–2.6
*Other tests	sometimes has a soapy feel
Crystal system	monoclinic or orthorhombic
Occurrence	widespread; mostly as large rock bodies formed by hydrothermal alteration of the ultramafic rocks dunite and pyroxenite; it may surround unaltered rocks; associated minerals are talc, magnesite, dolomite and chromite
Examples	Troodos Mountains (Cyprus), the Lizard, Cornwall (England), Saxony (Germany) and many locations in the USA

Talc $Mg_3Si_4O_{10}(OH)_2$

Talc is the softest mineral in Mohs'
scale of hardness, on which it is
listed as number 1. The massive variety
steatite, also called *soapstone* because of
its greasy feel, is an attractive, easily
worked form used for ornaments.
French chalk is a variety of steatite. Talc
has uses as a dry lubricant, as a filler in such
substances as paints, paper and rubber,
in cosmetics, and as an electrical and
thermal insulator. Cooking vessels
are made from soapstone. An allied
mineral *pyrophyllite*
($(Al_2Si_4O_{10}(OH)_2)$)
has similar
properties
and uses
as talc.

Foliated mass

pearly lustre

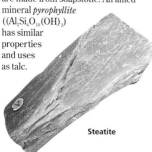

Steatite

Crystalline talc

TALC

*Colour	white, grey or pale green
Lustre	dull, pearly on cleavages
Transparency	translucent
*Hardness	1
Cleavage	basal perfect
Habit	foliated masses, sometimes in radiating groups; granular or compact
Specific gravity	2.6–2.8
*Other tests	soapy feel
Crystal system	monoclinic
Occurrence	forms as a secondary mineral by the alteration of olivine, pyroxene and amphibole and often accompanies serpentine in veins and faults in magnesium-rich rocks; sometimes formed by low-grade metamorphism of dolomitic limestones
Examples	Austria, India, South Africa, the Pyrenees, Korea and a number of places in the USA, Canada and the former USSR

This widely distributed form of silica is used in jewellery and for ornaments. There are several attractive varieties. *Rock crystal* is water-clear. *Milky quartz* is white. Colours are caused by impurities, such as ferric oxide in violet *amethyst*, manganese or titanium in *rose quartz*, and iron hydrates in yellow *citrine*. *Tiger's eye* is formed by fibrous inclusions of crocidolite. Tiny tourmaline, rutile and zoisite inclusions give *blue quartz*. *Rutilated quartz* contains needle-like yellow and red rutile crystals. *Aventurine quartz* contains scales of mica or goethite, giving a spangled green or brown look. Quartz is used in glass-making, ceramics, refractories, building materials and abrasives. Its piezoelectric property makes it useful in pressure-sensitive devices.

Rose quartz

QUARTZ

Colour	colourless or white with a wide range of tints
***Lustre**	vitreous
Transparency	transparent to translucent
***Hardness**	7
Cleavage	none
***Fracture**	conchoidal
***Habit**	crystals usually six-sided prisms terminated by six faces; prism faces horizontally striated
Twinning	very common but usually unobservable in hand specimen
Specific gravity	2.6
Crystal system	trigonal
Alteration	very stable to weathering
Occurrence	commonest mineral on the Earth's surface; in many acid igneous and metamorphic rocks, and in most clastic sediments; a common gangue mineral in veins and cavity fillings, where most good crystals specimens are found
Examples	ubiquitous; rock crystals in Brazil, France, Switzerland; smoky quartz in Scotland, and the Alps; citrine, rose quartz and amethyst in Brazil, aventurine quartz in Arizona (USA), San Cristobal (Mexico) and Rhineland (Germany)

Rock crystal

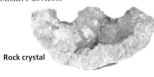

Citrine

Smoky quartz

Chalcedony SiO2

Chalcedony, the compact form of silica, is composed of microscopic quartz crystals. It is softer than quartz and denser than opal. The main types are *chalcedony*, which is uniformly coloured, and *agate*, which has curved bands or zones of varying colour. Chalcedony is a popular ornamental or gemstone. Varieties include the red to reddish brown, translucent *carnelian*, the red, opaque *jasper*, the apple-green *chrysoprase*, and *heliotrope*, which is green with red spots. *Flint* and *chert* are impure forms of chalcedony. *Onyx* is a variety of agate, with parallel layers of black and white. Chalcedony occurs in some fossils, such as petrified wood.

Agate

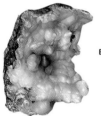

Botryoidal form

Stalactitic form

CHALCEDONY

Colour	variable, white to black via grey, red or brown shades
Lustre	waxy to vitreous
Transparency	transparent to substranslucent
Hardness	6.5
Cleavage	none
Fracture	conchoidal
*Habit	mostly botryoidal or stalactitic, often banded; lines cavities; massive or nodular
*Specific gravity	about 2.6
Crystal system	none, (cryptocrystalline)
*Occurrence	veins, cavity linings and masses in many different rock types; flint forms mainly in limestones
Examples	agate in Rio Grande do Sul (Brazil) and Idar-Oberstein (Germany); carnelian in Brazil, Uraguay and California (USA); chrysoprase in Queensland (Australia), the Urals (the former USSR) and California (USA); flint in the chalk of SE England (e.g. the white cliffs of Dover)

Opal is hydrated silica – that is, it contains about one-tenth (and sometimes as much as one-third) water. Opal is never crystalline, but it displays a rich play of colours, or 'fire', caused by the internal refraction of light by the arrays of tiny spheres of amorphous silica that make up the mineral. *Black opal*, which was once more precious than diamond, and the reddish *fire opal* are the most prized varieties. *Hydrophane* is a variety that becomes transparent when immersed in water. *Geyserite*, or *siliceous sinter*, is an opal deposited by hot springs and geysers. Opal forms the skeletons of some marine organisms, such as diatoms. *Diatomite* or *diatomaceous earth* is a sedimentary rock made up of the remains of diatoms.

Opal showing play of colours

Liver opal

Milk opal

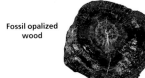

Fossil opalized wood

OPAL

Colour	variable; white, yellow, red, brown and others usually of pale shades
*Lustre	waxy or resinous
Transparency	transparent to subtranslucent
Hardness	5.5–6.5
Cleavage	none
Fracture	conchoidal
*Habit	massive, often stalactitic or rounded forms
Specific gravity	1.8–2.3
Crystal system	none, one of the few amorphous minerals
Occurrence	formed by weathering and alteration of siliceous rocks being deposited at low temperatures, especially in the area of geysers and hot springs; forms the skeletons of diatoms, radiolaria and sponges
Examples	in altered trachyte in the former Czechoslovakia and in sandstones of White Cliffs, NSW (Australia); fire opal at Queretaro (Mexico) and variously coloured in Transylvania (Romania); wood opal in Yellowstone National Park, Wyoming (USA) and Lake Omodeo (Sardinia)

Alkali Feldspars $KAlSi_3O_8$

Orthoclase
with tourmaline
and quartz

White microcline

Amazonstone

Orthoclase crystal

Sanidine, *orthoclase* and *microcline* are forms of alkali (or potassium) feldspars formed, respectively, at high, medium-to-high, and low temperatures. It is difficult to distinguish between orthoclase and microcline except when they are coloured. *Amazonite* is a green gem variety of microcline, while orthoclase often occurs as pink to red phenocrysts in granites. *Perthite* is an alkali feldspar, containing undulating layers of albite (a plagioclase feldspar) within individual crystals. The opposite phenomena of alkali feldspar lamellae in albite crystals are called *antiperthites*. *Adularia* is a colourless or white variety of orthoclase commonly found in pseudo-orthorhombic crystals. Some show an opalescent, white or blue play of colour. These are known as 'moonstones' and are used as gemstones. The alkali feldspars are important rock-forming minerals.

ALKALI FELDSPARS (POTASSIUM FELDSPARS)

*Colour	sanidine colourless to grey; orthoclase white to pink; microcline colourless to grey, sometimes green
Lustre	vitreous, pearly parallel to cleavage
Transparency	sanidine, transparent; orthoclase and microcline, transparent to translucent
*Hardness	6–6.5
*Cleavage	two perfect
Fracture	conchoidal to uneven
*Habit	sanidine tabular, prismatic crystals; orthoclase and microcline prismatic
Twinning	common
Specific gravity	2.5–2.6
Crystal system	sanidine and orthoclase are monoclinic, microcline is triclinic
Occurrence	sanidine forms phenocrysts in volcanic rocks and occurs in high-temperature metamorphic rocks; orthoclase is the commonest alkali feldspar of most igneous and metamorphic rocks; microcline occurs in granites, schists and gneisses and as grains in sedimentary rocks
Examples	the former Czechoslovakia for orthoclase; Sicily, Elba for sanidine; Colorado (USA) for amazonite

P lagioclase feldspars form a
continuous series ranging from
albite (NaAlSi₃O₈) through *oligoclase*,
andesine, *labradorite* and *bytownite* to
anorthite (CaAl₂Si₂O₈). Precise
classification is generally not possible in
hand specimens. Plagioclase feldspars
are distinguished from alkali feldspars by
striations on the cleavage surfaces
caused by the intersection of lamellar
twins with the cleavage surfaces.
Sunstone, a gem variety of oligoclase, is
usually reddish-brown or reddish-
orange, with a glitter effect caused by
aligned inclusions of iron minerals.
Labradorite shows a beautiful play of
colours. Like alkali feldspars, plagioclase
feldspars are important rock-forming
minerals.

Oligoclase
crystal

PLAGIOCLASE

Colour	white, greyish, pinkish or greenish; dark grey or blue-grey in some labradorites
Lustre	vitreous
Transparency	transparent to translucent
*Hardness	6–6.5
Cleavage	two good cleavages
Fracture	uneven
Habit	prismatic or tabular crystals; also massive, granular
*Twinning	repeated and simple twinning common and may occur together
Specific gravity	2.6–2.8
Other tests	labradorite often shows a play of blues and greens on cleavage surfaces
Crystal system	triclinic
Alteration	albite to kaolinite clay, more calcic minerals to a mixture of zoisite, calcite and albite
Occurrence	widely distributed; in many igneous rocks, sodic plagioclase in granite and calcic plagioclase in basalt and gabbro; albite in pegmatite and spilitic lavas
Examples	labradorite in anorthosites in Norway, Canada and the former USSR, fine specimens known as *spectrolite* in Finland; sunstone in pegmatites in Norway, Canada and the former USSR

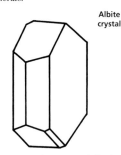

Albite
crystal

Labradorite

Nepheline *NaAlSiO₄*

Nepheline is a common feldspathoid mineral. (Feldspathoids are a group of rock-forming aluminosilicates similar to feldspars, but containing less silica.) It never occurs as a primary mineral associated with quartz in igneous rocks. The name nepheline comes from the Greek word for 'cloud', an allusion to the cloudiness observed when nepheline is placed in acid. Nepheline usually contains about 25 per cent of the 'potassium nepheline' *kalsilite* ($KAlSiO_4$) with which it forms a partial series. Kalsilite itself is very rare, being known only in some lavas on the Uganda-Zaire border. *Elaeolite* is a course-grained or massive, greenish, brownish or reddish nepheline with a greasy lustre. An associated mineral, *cancrinite*, is much less common. It tends to be yellow, yellow-brown or green and is rarely crystalline. Like nepheline, it is usually massive or occurs as grains. Nepheline is used in glass, ceramics and in the textile and oil industries. It is a minor ore of aluminium.

Massive form

vitreous lustre

NEPHELINE

Colour	usually colourless, white or grey, sometimes greenish or brown
Lustre	vitreous to greasy
Transparency	transparent to translucent
Hardness	6
Cleavage	poor
Fracture	conchoidal
Habit	rarely in six-sided prismatic crystals, usually massive
Specific gravity	2.6–2.7
*Other tests	gelatinizes in hydrochloric acid
Crystal system	hexagonal
Alteration	to white mica flakes; may alter to orange-red colours
Occurrence	in silica-poor igneous rocks, such as nepheline-syenites and phonolites (as an essential constituent mineral); rare basic volcanic rocks composed of nepheline and pyroxene are called nephelite, their intrusive equivalents are called ijolite
Examples	Kola Peninsula (the former USSR), Oslo (Norway), Bancroft (Canada), Maine and Arkansas (USA), Julianehaals district (Greenland) and East Africa

White crystals

Leucite is a member of the feldspathoid group of minerals. It is unstable under high pressures and does not occur in rocks that form underground by slow cooling. Hence, it appears only in lavas. The large crystals found in the lavas of Mount Vesuvius are a well-known example. The presence of feldspathoids such as leucite in an igneous rock precludes the presence of quartz. Thus these minerals form the basis of the classification of silica-poor rocks. The oval pinkish or white spots in some syenite rocks are thought to be 'pseudoleucites' – that is, the original leucite has changed to potassium feldspar and nepheline. Analcime and garnet share with leucite the perfect icositetrahedral crystal shape. But unlike leucite, analcime typically occurs in cavities, while garnet is not white or grey. Leucite has no real economic value although it has been used in the past as a source of potassium for fertilisers. The name leucite comes from the Greek word for 'white'.

Crystals in volcanic rock

Icositetrahedral crystal in volcanic rock

LEUCITE

Colour	white or ash-grey
Lustre	vitreous
Transparency	translucent
Streak	white
Hardness	5.5–6
Cleavage	very poor
Fracture	conchoidal
***Habit**	perfect trapezohedral (icositetrahedral) crystals; cubic aspect inherited from high-temperature crystallization
Twinning	very common, causing striations on crystal faces
Specific gravity	2.5
Crystal system	tetragonal below 625°C (1157°F), cubic above
Alteration	to a mixture of orthoclase and nepheline
***Occurrence**	only found in volcanic rocks and never in association with quartz; typically in potassium-rich, silica-poor lavas, such as trachytes
Examples	Mount Vesuvius and area around Rome (Italy), Bfumbira volcanic field (Uganda), Zaire, Eifel district (Germany), Leucite Hills, Wyoming (USA)

Sodalite $Na_8Al_6Si_6O_{24}Cl_2$

Sodalite occurs with other feldspathoids in silica-poor igneous rocks. Its blue forms are the best known. Also part of the sodalite group are *nosean* or *noselite* ($Na_8Al_6Si_6O_{24}(SO_4)$), and a calcium-containing type of nosean called *hauyne*. Both occur in alkali-rich volcanic rocks, such as phonolite. A better known related mineral is *lazurite* (($Na,Ca)_8(Al,Si)_{12}O_{24}(S,SO_4)$). Lazurite is a major constituent of *lapis lazuli*, which contains, alongside other associated minerals, small inclusions of pyrite. These inclusions not only make the rock attractive and valuable, but they also help to distinguish lazurite from blue sodalite.

Sodalite

SODALITE

*Colour	often blue, also white, pink or yellow
Lustre	vitreous or greasy
Transparency	transparent to translucent
Streak	white
Hardness	5.5–6
Cleavage	dodecahedral, poor
Fracture	conchoidal to uneven
Habit	crystals rare in dodecahedra; commonly massive, granular
Specific gravity	2.3
*Other tests	reddish fluorescence in ultraviolet light
Crystal system	cubic
*Occurrence	with nepheline and cancrinite in alkaline igneous rocks, such as nepheline syenites, and in some silica-poor lavas and dyke rocks
Examples	ditroite, a sodalite syenite from Ditrău (Romania) is a well-known example; others at Bancroft, Ontario and Ice River, British Columbia (Canada), Litchfield, Maine and Magnet Cove, Arkansas (USA) and Vesuvius (Italy)

Lapis lazuli

Haüyne in volcanic rock

Crystals in basalt

vesicles

Icositetrahedral crystals

Aggregate of crystals

A nalcime or analcite is one of a family of alumino-silicate minerals called zeolites. These minerals contain water molecules in spaces within the framework crystal lattice. The water may be expelled on heating. The name zeolite comes from the Greek words meaning 'to boil' and 'stone'. It refers to the fact that zeolites froth or boil when heated. Zeolites have many uses in industry, for example as catalysts and drying agents. Zeolites occur as low-grade metamorphic minerals, and also in vesicles (small cavities) in lavas, or in shallow igneous intrusions. Chemically and in crystal form and structure, analcime is closely related to leucite. It is distinguished by occurrence, as leucite is always embedded in the rock matrix. It is named after the Greek *analkes*, meaning 'weak', because of its weak pyroelectric properties when heated or rubbed.

ANALCIME

Colour	colourless, white or grey, may be tinted with yellow, green or pink
Lustre	vitreous
Transparency	transparent to nearly opaque
Streak	white
Hardness	5–5.5
Cleavage	imperfect, cubic
Fracture	uneven to conchoidal; brittle
Habit	usually in icositetrahedral crystals (as leucite), may be combined with cube
Specific gravity	2.2–2.4
Other tests	fuses to a colourless glass, colouring the flame yellow; decomposes in hydrochloric acid with the separation of silica; when rubbed or heated, becomes slightly charged
Crystal system	cubic
***Occurrence**	in cavities in basalt and dolerite affected by low temperature hydration and alteration, associated with other zeolites, calcite or prehnite; it may form in the early stages of metamorphism of volcanic glass in tuffaceous sandstones; a primary constituent of feldspathoidal basalts
Examples	Sicily, Austria, Iceland and the USA

125

Chabazite $CaAl_2Si_4O_{12}.6H_2O$

Red-brown rhombohedral crystals

White crystals

White crystals in basalt

Chabazite is a member of the zeolite family (see analcime). Like other zeolites, it occurs in vesicles, joints, cracks and fissures in basalts and other lavas. Chabazite and other zeolites are widely used to indicate temperature and depth of burial in ocean-floor basalts of the zeolite facies. Its rhombohedral crystals are an aid to identification. It can be distinguished from calcite by its poorer cleavage and because it does not effervesce in dilute hydrochloric acid. A variety of chabazite, called *phacolite*, occurs as colourless lenticular crystals produced by twinning. Chabazite is named from the Greek word for 'hailstone', which it resembles.

CHABAZITE

Colour	colourless, white, flesh pink, yellowish or brown
Lustre	vitreous
Transparency	transparent to translucent
Streak	white
Hardness	4–5
Cleavage	rhombohedral, imperfect
Fracture	uneven
*Habit	usually in cube-like rhombohedral crystals; crystals may be complex or twinned; also in compact masses
Twinning	common, interpenetrant
Specific gravity	2.1–2.2
Other tests	fuses to a nearly opaque whitish blebby glass; dissolves in hydrochloric acid with separation of silica
Crystal system	trigonal
Occurrence	in cavities and fissures in basalts, with other zeolites; also formed by chemical deposition from thermal waters
Examples	good crystals are found in Bolzano (Italy), the Cyclopean Islands (Sicily), and in cavities in granites in Elba (Italy); other well-known localities include the Faeroe Islands, Bohemia, Germany, Canada and the USA

$NaCa_2(Al_5Si_{13})O_{36}.14H_2O$ **Stilbite**

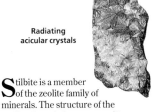

Radiating acicular crystals

Light brown crystals in basalt

Stilbite is a member of the zeolite family of minerals. The structure of the zeolites is such that structural ions may be replaced by the ions dissolved in the surrounding water. Thus the sodium ions in a sodium zeolite may be exchanged for the calcium in hard water. It typically occurs in cavities in basalts, often with another zeolite called *heulandite*. But while heulandite occurs in tabular crystals, twinned crystals of stilbite occur in a distinctive, sheaf-like form. Another distinguishing feature of both stilbite and heulandite is their lustre, which is pearly parallel to the cleavage, but vitreous elsewhere.

Pink crystal aggregate

STILBITE

Colour	white, sometimes yellowish or pink, may be brick-red
*Lustre	vitreous, pearly on cleavage surfaces
Transparency	transparent to translucent
Streak	white
Hardness	3.5–4
Cleavage	one perfect cleavage
Fracture	uneven
*Habit	as sheaf-like aggregates of twinned crystals, also as radial or globular aggregates
Twinning	common, giving cruciform, interpenetrant twins
Specific gravity	2.1–2.2
Other tests	soluble in hydrochloric acid, and fuses easily to an opaque white glass
Crystal system	monoclinic
Occurrence	in cavities in amygdaloidal basalts, often with heulandite and calcite; also in granites, schists and ore deposits; also found in the early stages of metamorphism of tuffaceous sandstones
Examples	good crystals in New Jersey (USA), Kilpatrick and Isle of Skye (Scotland), Nova Scotia (Canada), Rio Grande do Sul (Brazil) and in Iceland; also found in granites in Italy, Austria, Sweden, India and in the USA

Granites

Granites are coarse-grained rocks with a mottled appearance. They comprise a mixture of glassy quartz, white, pink or red alkali feldspar, minor amounts of dark minerals, and often white, sodic plagioclase. Their low density and resistance to weathering means that they usually form high, rugged terrains. Quarrymen use the term granite for almost any hard rock. Geologists use it either in a restricted sense, or as a blanket term for granitoids of acid or intermediate composition. Their complex and varied origins give rise to a great variety of types. Weather-resistant stones are polished for use as decorative facings on buildings. Granites that weather to pure kaolin provide china clay.

Biotite granite

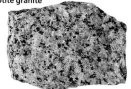

Graphic granite

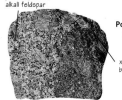

phenocrysts of alkali feldspar

Porphyritic granite

xenolith of basic rock

Hornblende biotite granite

GRANITES

Colour	colourless grains, also mottled in white, pink or red; grey or dark grains
Colour index	5–20
Mineralogy	essential quartz, alkali feldspar and plagioclase in variable amounts, with hornblende and/or biotite; muscovite may occur
Texture	coarse-grained; usually granular; may be porphyritic with phenocrysts of feldspar; sometimes foliated; coarse intergrowths of quartz and feldspars can form a 'graphic' texture
Structure	commonly contain xenoliths, may contain cavities (druses) into which well-formed crystals project; may be associated wth much late-stage mineralization
Classification	acid plutonic igneous rock QAPF field 3 (and 2 – alkali feldspar granite)
Alteration	usually quite resistant to weathering, but can give clay minerals and quartz sand; can show hydrothermal or pneumatolytic alteration
Occurrence	intrusive, most commonly occurring in batholiths
Examples	England, Scotland, SE Asia, Peru, Greenland, Australia

Granodiorite

Granodiorite

Granodiorite is a coarse-grained intrusive igneous rock. It is similar to granite in composition, but contains less alkali feldspar. As a result, it does not usually show the reddish colour of some granites, even when weathered, but is normally greyish white. It is the most common coarse-grained igneous rock, occurring as plutons in mountain-building regions, where it is often associated with other igneous rock types, such as diorite or granite. It also occurs in dykes. The US geologist George Becker was the first person to use the term on maps of the Gold Belt of the Sierra Nevada, California.

GRANODIORITE

Colour	greyish white
Colour index	usually 5–25
Mineralogy	essential quartz, plagioclase, and lesser amounts of alkali feldspar, with minor amounts of hornblende and biotite; may also contain pyroxene or muscovite
Texture	coarse-grained; grains approximately of equal size (granular texture); mafic minerals may show some crystal faces (subhedral); occasionally porphyritic, phenocrysts of alkali feldspar; may show orbicular texture
Classification	intermediate plutonic igneous rock QAPF field 4
Occurrence	the most voluminous of all plutonic rocks, occurring in the same environments as granite; they form large areas within Precambrian gneissose massifs and plutons within orogenic belts; associated rocks are diorites, quartz diorites and sometimes granites
Examples	Donegal (Ireland), Leicestershire (England); Caledonian mountain belt, Scandinavia and Cordilleran belt of western North America

Granodiorite

Pegmatite

Pegmatite

feldspar

Pegamatite

This distinctive rock is often light in colour and extremely coarse, though grain sizes vary greatly. Pegmatite bodies range in size from centimetres to thousands of metres. They occur widely in both stable areas and in younger continental mountain belts. Although commonly composed of the same minerals found in most igneous rocks, they may also contain rare minerals. They may be economically valuable as sources of mica, silica and gemstones, including emerald and topaz. Pegmatites also form a source for metals and raw materials used in the ceramic, electronic and nuclear power industries.

Pegmatite

mica

PEGMATITE

Colour	variable, depending on constituents
Mineralogy	commonly quartz or alkali feldspar, but can be those of any igneous rock type; may contain less common minerals, such as beryl, topaz or tourmaline; apatite, beryl, garnet, magnetite, topaz and zircon sparse but widespread
Texture	notable for very coarse grain-size, average 10 cm (4 in) but variable over short distances; mica and quartz crystals may be 1–3 m (3–10 ft) across, feldspar crystals (2–10 m) (6–33 ft); textures similar to those of common igneous rocks, but on a much larger scale; often equi-granular with grains of irregular shape; also porphyritic; some bodies may be zoned; may contain cavities a few centimetres wide with beautifully formed crystals of gem quality
Examples	Precambrian terrain of Fennoscandia, deposits with rare minerals at Varutrask (Sweden); pegmatitic pyroxenites at the base of the Merensky Reef (South Africa)

Dacite

Porphyritic dacite

Dacite

Dacite is the volcanic equivalent of granodiorite and tonalite, two intrusive rocks. Geologists use the term dacite for rocks containing between 63 and 69 per cent silica, which comprise at least 10 per cent quartz, and plagioclase feldspar (An less than 70 per cent). They may also contain minor amounts of biotite, hornblende and pyroxene. Dacites, together with andesites, are the most characteristic, if not the most abundant, volcanic rocks that are formed by volcanic action in mountain-building regions. The lava is extremely viscous and tends to form steep-sided flows, often with platy jointing or a block-like structure. It may also form domes or occur as pyroclastic rocks.

DACITE

Colour	medium grey
Colour index	less than 20
Mineralogy	quartz and sodic plagioclase with minor amounts of biotite and/or hornblende and/or pyroxene
Texture	often porphyritic, with phenocrysts of plagioclase, augite or hypersthene, or rarely olivine; may form glassy or highly vesiculated rocks
Structure	may show flow-banding, also found as ignimbrites
Classification	intermediate volcanic QAPF fields 4 and 5
Occurrence	more common in orogenic and continental settings than in oceanic regions, forming chains of composite volcanoes, may also occur as domes on the upper flanks of large, mature volcanoes; may be associated with earthquakes
Examples	found as islands and on the continental margins around the Pacific Ocean, Indonesia and the Lesser Antilles; ignimbrites in the Great Basin (USA), in plateau regions of Mexico and C America; the northern margins of the Alpine System

Rhyolite

Flow-banded rhyolite

Rhyolite

R hyolite, an acid volcanic rock, is the chemical equivalent of granite but with finer grains. Light in colour and in weight, it may resemble flint. It often shows a banding of colour or texture, known as *flow banding*. This is caused by the flow of the lava and is commonly contorted. Rhyolites may also show spherulitic texture – containing spherical bodies less than 0.5 cm (0.2 in) across. They contain radially arranged, needle-like crystals, often of quartz or feldspar. Rhyolite magma is stiffer and flows less easily than basalt lava. As a result, it only occasionally reaches the Earth's surface.

Flow-banded rhyolite

RHYOLITE

Colour	white, greenish, grey, brownish or reddish
Mineralogy	quartz, alkali feldspar and plagioclase (oligoclase or albite), also glass of equivalent composition; mafic minerals include augite, hypersthene, iron-rich olivine (fayalite), biotite, magnetite and ilmenite
Texture	fine-grained or glassy, may contain phenocrysts of quartz, alkali feldspar, hornblende or mica in a microcrystalline groundmass
Structure	flow-banding may occur; more glassy types may show irregular or spheroidal fractures; may develop spherulitic or vesicular texture, the vesicles sometimes being filled to form amygdales; commonly brecciated, the main constituent of volcanic ash
Classification	acid volcanic igneous rock QAPF field 3
Occurrence	as plugs in volcanic vents, or short, thick flows, or as domes up to hundreds of metres across; rhyolitic eruptions are associated with strato-volcanoes
Examples	Iceland, Jersey

O bsidian, a volcanic glass formed by rapid cooling, has the same composition as dacite or rhyolite, with less than 1 per cent water. It is typically black and glassy, with a *conchoidal* (shell-like) fracture. The black colour appears because of the way the embryonic crystals in the glass scatter the light. Obsidian may be red-brown due to the presence of iron, and greenish or grey due to the presence of tiny gas bubbles. Shattered fragments of obsidian have sharp edges and it was once used to make implements and weapons. Especially prized are such varieties as snow-flake obsidian, which contains small, grey spherulites, and the silky lustred obsidian of Mexico.

Obsidian

conchoidal fracture

vesicles

Obsidian

vitreous lustre

Obsidian

OBSIDIAN

Colour	black, greenish black, grey or red-brown
Mineralogy	mostly glassy, of equivalent composition to rhyolite or granite
Texture	none; glassy, although may contain less than 1 per cent minute crystals (microlites); may contain minute crystals of quartz, feldspar, pyroxene or magnetite
Structure	glass may contain spherical bodies (spherulites) ranging from microscopic to over a metre; perlitic cracks may be present; may be spotted or show flow-banding; breaks with a conchoidal fracture
Classification	acid or intermediate volcanic igneous rock
Alteration	hydrates to form perlite, a grey, pearly-lustred volcanic glass, which characteristically has an intricate network of concentric cracks resembling an onion
Occurrence	not widely distributed, although the commonest of natural glasses; formed when acid or intermediate lava is cooled very rapidly; occurs as flows and dykes, associated with rhyolite
Examples	USA, England, Italy, Iceland, Japan, Java

133

Pitchstone

Pitchstone, a volcanic glass, is formed when dacitic or rhyolitic lava is rapidly chilled on or near the Earth's surface. It is black, brown or red, with a resinous lustre resembling that of pitch. It is similar to obsidian, but it contains more crystalline material. This may comprise quartz, alkali or plagioclase feldspar, or pyroxene phenocrysts. Pitchstone is of a duller appearance than obsidian, because it contains more water (between 4 and 10 per cent). The origin of the water is not understood. It also has an irregular, hackly fracture, unlike the conchoidal fracture of obsidian. Pitchstone occurs at the base of acid lava flows or it may form the margins of intrusive dykes and sills.

Pitchstone

resinous lustre

PITCHSTONE

Colour	dark coloured, black brown or grey
Mineralogy	mostly glassy, but crystalline material may be quartz, alkali or plagioclase feldspar, pyroxene; may also contain iron-rich olivine (fayalite)
Texture	glassy, but contains more crystalline material than obsidian; phenocrysts common, of quartz and feldspar or even light green pyroxene
Structure	flow structure common (see obsidian); perlitic structure also occurs, caused by tension set up during contraction on cooling; breaks with an irregular fracture
Classification	acid or intermediate volcanic igneous rock
Occurrence	as flows and dykes, commonly associated with rhyolites
Examples	Islands of Arran and Eigg (Scotland), Shropshire and Devon (England), Meissen (Germany), Pantelleria (Italy), Hlinik (Hungary), Lugano (Switzerland)

Pitchstone

phenocrysts

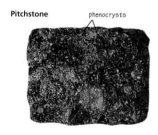

Pitchstone

P umice is a pale grey, frothy volcanic glass, usually of acid composition, although it can also be intermediate or mafic. It is an extremely light, porous rock, containing 50 to 75 per cent gas. Some types are so light that they float on water. *Scoria* is a mafic glass, similar to pumice, but denser. The vesicles are larger and more spherical in form, giving it an open cellular structure. Pumice is used as an abrasive. When mixed with cement, it makes a useful, lightweight building material. Pumice and ash erupted from volcanoes is sometimes transported by wind for thousands of kilometres. The thin deposit of ash and pumice – *tephra* – is useful in correlating different rocks of the same age.

vesicles

Pumice

PUMICE

Colour	very light grey, or yellowish
Mineralogy	glass, but with accessory crystals of various silicates (e.g. sanidine, oligoclase), quartz, biotite, zeolites and calcite
Texture	highly vesicular; many protuberances and vacuoles, which make it very light
Structure	vacuoles may be oriented due to flow; may occur as fragments less than 1 cm (0.4 in) across, often flattened, in ignimbrites; scoria has an open cellular structure
Classification	volcanic igneous rock, usually of acid composition, but can be intermediate or mafic
Occurrence	usually formed during explosive volcanic eruptions, but may also form by quieter bubbling at the top of lava flows; it may be carried on the wind for thousands of kilometres from the source volcano
Examples	Lipari Islands, Vesuvius (Italy), e.g. during the eruption of AD 79 which destroyed Pompeii; most of the volcanoes of Suna (Indonesia) and Japan

Basaltic scoria

Pumice breccia

Diorite

Diorite is a coarse-grained plutonic igneous rock, composed of 50 to 75 per cent plagioclase feldspar, and dark-coloured minerals. They are mottled dark grey and white rocks, the mafic minerals tending to look darker than in gabbros. With increasing quartz content, it first becomes *quartz diorite* and then *tonalite*. If alkali feldspar forms more than 10 per cent of the feldspar, it is known as *monzodiorite*. Diorite is distinguished from gabbro on the composition of the plagioclase feldspar (An less than 50 per cent), and also on colour index. Most gabbros have a colour index greater than 40, while anorthosites have a colour index of less than 10. Polished slabs of diorite are used as building stones. The name diorite is derived from the Greek words meaning 'to distinguish'.

Diorite

Diorite

Diorite

DIORITE

Colour	dark grey and white
Colour index	25–50
Mineralogy	sodic plagioclase, commonly hornblende and often with biotite or augite; may also contain minor amounts of quartz and alkali feldspar (less than 10 per cent each)
Texture	medium- to coarse-grained; where medium-grained, known as *microdiorite*, most of which are porphyritic, although some are equigranular
Structure	often contains fine-grained basic inclusions; occasionally shows orbicular structure
Classification	intermediate plutonic igneous rock QAPF field 10 (and 5–tonalite, 9–monzodiorite)
Occurrence	occurs in association with gabbro, tonalite, granodiorite and granite as part of the great granitic intrusions known as batholiths within continental crust
Examples	Nuneaton (England), Esbo (Finland), Laugendal (Norway), Ortles Alps (Italy), Orno (Sweden), Peru, Southern California batholith (USA)

Andesite

Andesite, named after the South American Andes, is the intermediate volcanic equivalent of diorite. It is a fine-grained or partly glassy rock, differing from basalt in its lower colour index. Andesites and dacites are the most characteristic, if not the most abundant volcanic rocks in mountain-building regions, forming chains of volcanic islands or ranges close to continental margins. They also occur in continental interiors. The viscous lavas erupt, often quite violently, from chains of composite volcanoes and are associated with deep earthquakes. Lava flows are steep-sided, often showing platy jointing and a blocky structure.

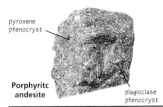

pyroxene phenocryst

Porphyritic andesite

plagioclase phenocryst

Augite andesite

Andesite

brown surface weathering

ANDESITE

Colour	blackish brown or greenish
Colour index	less than 35
Mineralogy	plagioclase (often zoned from labradorite to oligoclase), pyroxene, hornblende and/or biotite
Texture	usually porphyritic, phenocrysts commonly plagioclase, augite or hypersthene, occasionally olivine
Structure	blocky, showing platy jointing
Classification	intermediate volcanic igneous rock QAPF 9 and 10
Occurrence	in orogenic (mountain-building) environments i.e. in island arcs and active continental margins; also in continental settings
Examples	common on islands and continental margins of the circum-Pacific region, an 'Andesite Line' separating the lines of volcanoes from the interior of the ocean which is free of volcanism; Indonesia and the Lesser Antilles; Colorado Plateau (USA), Mexico, Central America (continental setting); in Europe, found along the northern margins of the Alps, especially the Carpathian Mountains and N Turkey

Syenite

Sodalite syenite — sodalite

Nepheline syenite — nepheline

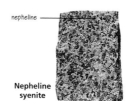

Syenite

S yenite is an intermediate intrusive igneous rock in which the dominant mineral is alkali feldspar. It was named after Syene, the old Greek name for Aswan, in southern Egypt, although the rock in this area is actually a hornblende granite. A closely related type of rock, known as *alkali feldspar syenite*, is especially striking. It is called *larvikite* after a type found in Larvik, Norway. It contains iridescent alkali feldspars. Known as 'pale Labrador', it is highly decorative and polished slabs are used as building stone. Larvikite has been found in the boulder clays of East Anglia, England and is thought to have been transported there by an ice sheet during the Pleistocene. Another related rock is nepheline syenite. This, like syenite, is uncommon.

SYENITE

Colour	red, pink, grey or white
Colour index	10–35
Mineralogy	alkali feldspar dominant, with subordinate sodic plagioclase, biotite, pyroxene, amphibole and sometimes iron olivine (fayalite); may also contain minor quartz or nepheline
Texture	coarse to medium-grained; commonly subhedral granular, but tabular feldspar crystals may have a subparallel orientation; occasionally porphyritic
Structure	drusy structure may be present
Classification	intermediate plutonic igneous rock QAPF field 7 (and 6–alkali feldspar syenite)
Occurrence	as stocks, dykes or sills, or around granodiorite plutons; alkali syenites (and their extrusive equivalent trachyte) are the most abundant rock type in many continental alkaline provinces; associated rocks include alkali granite or nepheline syenite, also alkali gabbro; the most important setting is that of crustal extension
Examples	Germany, African rift systems; British Columbia (Canada); Maine (USA)

Trachyte

Trachyte

Trachyte

alkali feldspar
phenocrysts

Trachytes are the volcanic equivalent of syenites. Their name comes from the Greek word *trachys*, meaning 'rough', an allusion to their surface roughness. They give rise to the fluidal texture called *trachytic*. Trachytes occur not only as lavas, but also as pyroclastic rocks. These include tuff, pumice flows and ignimbrites with a streaky or blotched appearance due to the alternation of lenses and bands of different colours, composition or texture. Trachyte is used for paving and flooring, because rubbing does not make it shiny. It is also used as a facing stone on buildings.

Trachyte

feldspar phenocryst

Trachyte

feldspar
phenocryst

TRACHYTE

Colour	usually grey, may be white, pink or yellowish
Mineralogy	essential alkali feldspar; may contain quartz (quartz trachyte) or feldspathoid (feldspathoid-bearing trachyte); if containing alkali pyroxene or amphibole, it is called alkali trachyte
Texture	fine-grained, usually with phenocrysts of one or two feldspars; tabular feldspars in the matrix may show parallel orientation due to flow (trachytic texture); groundmass glass may occur
Structure	may be vesicular or agglomeratic
Classification	intermediate volcanic QAPF field 7 (and 6–alkali trachyte)
Occurrence	a comparatively rare but persistent member of oceanic basaltic suites, may be extruded with rhyolite from the same volcano; occurs as lava flows and very commonly as volcanic domes or plugs
Examples	Drachenfels, Siebengebirge (Germany), Puy de Dôme, Auvergne (central France), Tahiti (Pacific Islands), St. Helena and Ascension (S Atlantic)

Gabbro

Olivine gabbro

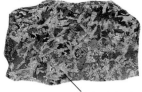

lath-shaped plagioclase

Troctolite

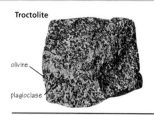

olivine

plagioclase

Layered gabbro

Gabbros are basic intrusive igneous rocks, subdivided according to the relative abundances of orthopyroxene, clinopyroxene, olivine and hornblende. Varieties include *norite* (plagioclase and orthopyroxene), *troctolite* or *troutstone*, so-called because of its spotted appearance (plagioclase and olivine), and *hornblende gabbro* (plagioclase and hornblende with a little pyroxene). Gabbro differs from diorite on the composition of the plagioclase feldspar (An greater than 50 per cent). It is an important member of the ophiolite suite, or rocks representing ancient ocean floor. In this setting, it is affected by low-grade metamorphism. Gabbros are occasionally used as facing stones on buildings, especially the attractive dark varieties, but it is too fragile to make a good construction material.

GABBRO

Colour	grey to black, speckled with white; troctolite may have black, brown or reddish spots
Colour index	35–65
Mineralogy	essential calcic plagioclase, pyroxene and iron oxides; may contain olivine (olivine gabbro) or quartz (quartz gabbro); varieties may contain orthopyroxene and/or hornblende
Texture	coarse-grained; often subhedral granular, may show poikilitic or subophitic texture in which plates of pyroxene partly enclose plagioclase crystals; lath-like crystals of feldspar may be aligned parallel to layering
Structure	commonly layered, may show alternating light (feldspar-rich) and dark (pyroxene and/or olivine-rich) layers; may show pegmatitic segregations
Classification	basic plutonic igneous rock QAPF field 10
Occurrence	typical of layered intrusions, especially ophiolites, but also in thick sills
Examples	USA, Canada and South Africa; troctolite on Rhum (Scotland) and Germany; norite in S Norway

Dolerite

Dolerite

olerite is a basic intrusive igneous rock, intermediate in grain size between basalt and gabbro. In North America and Europe, it is often called *diabase*, though many people restrict this term for dolerite which has been altered. In industry, dolerite is called *whin*, *whinstone*, *trap* or *traprock*. Dolerites occur as hypabyssal bodies – that is, they are intrusions of smaller grain size and dimensions than plutons, and they form dykes and sills. They are important members of the ophiolite suite, representing ancient oceanic crust. Such 'dyke swarms' represent the repeated intrusion of magma at mid-ocean ridges. In this setting, they are weakly metamorphosed. It is used locally as a building stone. The smaller grain size gives a less fragile rock than gabbro. Dolerites are usually quite uniform bodies but can diversify more than basalts. Such diversification can be caused by the settling of more dense crystals, such as olivine. This is seen more often in sills than in dykes.

Dolerite

DOLERITE

Colour	black, dark grey or green when fresh; may be mottled black and white
Mineralogy	essential plagioclase, pyroxene and opaque minerals; may contain olivine (olivine dolerite) or quartz (quartz dolerite)
Texture	medium grain size; ophitic texture common; quickly cooled varieties show porphyritic texture with phenocrysts of plagioclase, pyroxene, and sometimes olivine; may contain glass in the groundmass
Structure	may show layering, patches or veins of dolerite pegmatite, also small amounts of glass; vesicles and amygdales may occur
Classification	basic intrusive igneous rock QAPF field 10
Occurrence	as dykes or sills, sometimes forming swarms which may comprise hundreds or thousands of individual bodies, which may radiate out from a single volcanic centre
Examples	widespread; forms a great belt of Mesozoic intrusions extending from Tasmania and parts of S Australia across Antarctica and into South Africa

Basalt

Vesicular basalt

vesicles

amygdales

Amygdaloidal basalt

Basalt

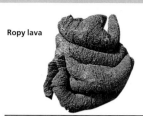

Ropy lava

Basalts are basic volcanic igneous rocks. They are extremely abundant not only on Earth, where they have erupted throughout known geologic history, but also on the Moon where they formed before the Moon became quiescent 2.5 to 3 billion years ago. Basalts are fine-grained, dark-coloured rocks, essentially composed of plagioclase feldspar and pyroxene. The many types vary according to their chemistry and mineralogy. They include *alkali basalt*, *mid-ocean ridge basalt* (MORB), *olivine basalt* and *tholeiite*. Basalt is distinguished from andesite by its higher colour index (greater than 35). Basalt may show columnar jointing, forming hexagonal pillars of rock. A particularly good example is the 'Giant's Causeway' in Northern Ireland. Basalt is used for road paving and as ballast for roads and railways.

BASALT

Colour	black when fresh, may be altered to form a greenish or reddish crust
Colour index	greater than 35
Mineralogy	essential calcic plagioclase and pyroxene; olivine and minor feldspathoids or quartz may be present
Texture	fine grain-size, may have phenocrysts of olivine, pyroxene or plagioclase
Structure	commonly vesicular or amygdaloidal, filled with zeolites, carbonate or silica; may contain olivine- or pyroxene-bearing xenoliths; may form columnar joints on cooling; surface forms of lava flows may be rough and clinkery (*aa*) or have a ropy appearance (*pahoehoe*); submarine lava flows show pillow structure
Classification	basic volcanic igneous rock QAPF fields 9 and 10
Occurrence	forms lava flows either in shallow shield volcanoes or as sheets forming huge lava plateaux; forms the bulk of the ocean floor as well as oceanic volcanoes, islands and floor rift valleys; also dykes and sills
Examples	USA, Australia, the former USSR, East African Rift, NW Europe and Hawaii

Anorthosite

Anorthosites are medium- to coarse-grained igneous rocks, composed of at least 90 per cent plagioclase feldspar. The *layered type*, composed of bytownite (plagioclase feldspar An_{70-90}), occurs in large layered complexes of any age from Precambrian to late Tertiary. The *massif type*, composed of andesine or labradorite (An_{30-70}), occurs only in Precambrian gneissose rocks between 1,000 and 1,700 years old. A third type occurs in gneissose bands in high-grade metamorphic rocks. Anorthosites, more than 4 billion years old, are important on the Moon. Anorthosites composed of labradorite show an iridescent display of colours.

Anorthosite

ANORTHOSITE

Colour	white or light grey
Colour index	0–10
Mineralogy	essential plagioclase, often with small amounts of pyroxene
Texture	medium or coarse-grained; feldspar crystals usually over 1 cm (0.4 in) in size, but may range up to 1 m (3.3 ft) and often aligned; pyroxene crystals sparse, but may be very large
Structure	may be banded in grain size and texture
Classification	plutonic igneous rock QAPF field 10
Occurrence	either as layers in large, mafic intrusions where they are associated with gabbros, troctolites and norites, or as 'massif type anorthosites' in the form of large independent intrusions, characteristically in Precambrian gneiss terrains
Examples	in layered intrusions at Skaergaard (Greenland), Stillwater, Montana (USA), Bushveld (South Africa) and Muskox (Canada); massif type anorthosites in Quebec (Canada), the Adirondacks, New York (USA) and Scandinavia

Anorthosite

labradorite —

Anorthosite

143

Pyroxenite

Pyroxenite

Clinopyroxenite

Orthopyroxenite

Pyroxenites are ultramafic plutonic rocks. They consist of essential pyroxene, together with up to 40 per cent olivine. They include *clinopyroxenites* (made up almost entirely of clinopyroxene), *orthopyroxenites* (made up almost entirely of orthopyroxene) and *websterites* (containing equal proportions of each). As the amount of olivine increases, they grade into peridotites. Although ultramafic because dark constituents make up more than 90 per cent, pyroxenites are chemically basic because they contain more than 44 per cent silica. There are no true volcanic equivalents of pyroxenites.

PYROXENITE

Colour	green, dark green, dark brown or black
Colour index	greater than 90
Mineralogy	essential pyroxene, up to 40 per cent olivine; websterite contains equal amounts of ortho- and clinopyroxene; may also contain hornblende, micas, garnet, feldspar, spinel, ilmenite and sulphides
Texture	medium- to coarse-grained, granular
Structure	may occur as layers, with oriented crystals
Classification	ultramafic, basic plutonic igneous rock
Occurrence	as small independent intrusions (stocks or dykes); present as nodules in basalts, nephelinites and kimberlites; as individual layers in layered gabbros, and in the ultramafic portions of ophiolite complexes
Examples	websterite in Webster County, North Carolina (USA), Troodos Ophiolite Complex (Cyprus), Stillwater Complex, Montana (USA), Bushveld (South Africa), Great Dyke (Zimbabwe), Tulameen district, British Columbia (Canada), Monte Somma, Vesuvius (Italy)

Peridotite

P eridotite is a term used for all ultramafic plutonic igneous rocks that consist essentially of olivine with pyroxene and/or amphibole. The four main types, depending on the relative proportions of the constituent minerals, are *dunite* (more than 90 per cent olivine – see dunite), *harzburgite*, *lherzolite* and *wehrlite*. All contain more than 40 per cent olivine. Peridotites are found in large amounts at the base of ophiolite complexes. Smaller amounts may occur as inclusions in other rocks, representing parts of the mantle. They may also contain biotite and small amounts of garnet and/or spinel. Peridotite has been recovered from the Moon, as blocks in breccias which are thought to represent material from the gabbro-anorthosite Lunar Highlands.

Peridotite

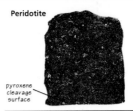

pyroxene cleavage surface

PERIDOTITE

Colour	dull green to black (see also dunite)
Colour index	greater than 90
Mineralogy	essential olivine and orthopyroxene (harzburgite); olivine with minor ortho- and clinopyroxene (lherzolite); essential olivine and clinopyroxene (wehrlite); common accessory minerals are hornblende, mica, spinel, garnet, feldspar
Texture	granular; also poikilitic, with large crystals of one type enclosing smaller crystals of another
Structure	layering may be present
Classification	ultramafic plutonic igneous rock
Alteration	may alter to serpentine minerals
Occurrence	the major component of the Earth's mantle, and a minor but important component of the Earth's crust; at the Earth's surface, it occurs as mantle-derived inclusions in basalts, nephelinites or kimberlites, and in the lower part of ophiolite complexes
Examples	harzburgite in Harz Mountains (Germany); lherzolite at Lhers, Ariège and in Pyrenees (France)

Plagioclase-bearing wehrlite

plagioclase

Wehrlite

Dunite

Dunite, a variety of peridotite, contains more than 90 per cent olivine. It occurs within linear or *en echelon* bodies known as ultramafic belts, often in association with gabbros, dolerite dykes in parallel sheets, pillow lavas of basalt, and greywackes. This type of complex is known as an *ophiolite suite*, and probably represents an ancient oceanic floor. Dunite also occurs in the cores of stock-like intrusions, which are surrounded by peridotite, pyroxenite, hornblende-magnetite pyroxenite, and an outermost zone of basic rocks. Olivine crystals are thought to accumulate to form dunite because they are formed in the early stages of cooling and have a high density.

Dunite nodule

Dunite

brown weathered surface

Dunite

DUNITE

Colour	light to dark green, or shades of yellow and brown
Colour index	more than 90
Mineralogy	essential olivine (more than 90 per cent); may contain accessory orthopyroxene, clinopyroxene or chromite
Texture	medium- to coarse-grained; granular, often sugary texture
Structure	forms xenoliths, lenses and masses
Classification	ultramafic plutonic igneous rock
Alteration	usually altered, partly or completely, to serpentinite
Occurrence	as nodules in basalts; at the base of layered intrusions; associated with other ultramafic rocks at the base of ophiolite complexes; forming the core of concentrically zoned stocks
Examples	Dun Mountain, Nelson (New Zealand); in zoned stocks in SE Alaska; in ophiolite complexes, such as Troodos (Cyprus); often associated with harzburgite, a type of peridotite; Gorgona Island (Columbia); at the base of layered intrusions in Stillwater, Montana (USA) and Bushveld (South Africa)

Carbonatite

Carbonatite

Carbonatite

Rare earth
carbonatite

Rare earth
carbonatite

Carbonatites, igneous rocks containing more than 50 per cent carbonates, are either plutonic (intrusive) or volcanic (extrusive) in origin. The varieties depend on the nature of the carbonate present, namely calcite, dolomite or other, more unusual carbonates of sodium, calcium and potassium. Carbonate tuffs have provided excellent environments for the rapid fossilization of land animals. They include well-preserved footprints at Laetoli, Tanzania. A number of mineral deposits, including apatite, copper, fluorite, magnetite, pyrochlore and vermiculite, occur in carbonatites. They are also the world's largest source of rare earth elements.

CARBONATITE

Colour	light, greyish or yellowish
Mineralogy	largely composed of carbonate minerals, principally calcite and dolomite; may also contain accessory minerals
Texture	grain-size can be fine, medium or coarse
Structure	intrusives form plugs, dykes and cone-sheets; volcanics form unstable lavas and pyroclastic deposits
Classification	volcanic or plutonic igneous rock
Alteration	superficially cavernous through solution
Occurrence	found as subvolcanic intrusions and as lavas and tuffs, mostly in the stable interiors of continents; most form carbonatite complexes with alkaline and/or ultrabasic volcanic rocks and country rocks affected by intense potassium and/or sodium metasomatism
Examples	Norway, Sweden, the USA, Malawi; a rock bearing sodium, potassium and calcium carbonates is found at Ol Doinyo Lengai volcano (Tanzania); rare earth carbonatite at Mountain Pass, California (USA)

Phonolite

Nepheline phonolite

Nosean phonolite

nosean phenocrysts

Phonolite

PHONOLITE

Colour	dark green to grey, with a greasy lustre
Colour index	0–30
Mineralogy	essential alkali feldspar and feldspathoids; may contain pyroxenes and amphiboles, usually sodic varieties
Texture	fine-grained, with or without phenocrysts of feldspar, nepheline or, less commonly, leucite; rarely partly glassy; may show trachytic texture (see trachyte)
Structure	may be fissile (splits into flat sheets); can be vesicular, or show small scale drusy structure, sometimes lined with late stage minerals
Classification	alkaline intermediate volcanic igneous rock QAPF field 11
Occurrence	forms lava flows, sills and dykes; characteristically in continental rift settings, may be associated with basic and acid extrusive rocks, sometimes carbonatite; also a minor component of oceanic olivine basalt-trachyte associations
Examples	Rift Valley (East Africa), Gardar Rift Province (Greenland) and Tenerife; leucite phonolite in C Italy

Phonolite, a fine-grained intermediate igneous rock, was once called *clinkstone*, because of the ringing sound it is supposed to make when hit with a hammer. It is the extrusive equivalent of feldspathoidal syenite. It does not contain enough silica to crystallize quartz and forms some feldspathoid minerals rather than all feldspar – feldspathoid plus silica equates to feldspar. The most usual feldspathoid is nepheline. Others, including leucite, nosean, hauyne, sodalite or analcime, may also be present. Phonolites occur not only as fine-grained lavas, but also as glassy rocks, pyroclastic rocks, pumice deposits and ash-flow deposits. As with other alkaline rocks phonolites occur in continental rifts, the most important deposits occuring in the Kenya Rift Valley in Africa.

Lamprophyre

Lamprophyre

Lamprophyre is the name for a distinctive group of igneous rocks characterized by dark minerals with a marked porphyritic texture. They form dykes or small intrusions, and commonly show hydrothermal alteration. The name comes from the Greek word *lampros*, meaning 'glistening'. These rocks are not simply variations of common igneous rock, but they have an unusual mineralogy and chemistry, with higher concentrations of water, carbon dioxide, sulphur, phosphorus, strontium, barium and certain trace elements than other rocks of similar composition. Lamprophyres have restricted occurrence and are usually associated with granites, diorites and syenites.

Lamprophyre

Lamprophyre

LAMPROPHYRE

Colour	dark, lustrous rocks
Colour index	35–90
Mineralogy	essential biotite and/or amphibole, also clinopyroxene and olivine; feldspars and/or feldspathoids, when present, are restricted to the groundmass; may contain calcite and zeolites
Texture	generally even-grained, with well-shaped crystals; may be porphyritic, with mafic (dark-coloured) minerals occurring as phenocrysts and in the groundmass
Structure	may contain xenocrysts, or xenoliths of mantle of deep crustal origin; ocellar structure common, ocelli being small rounded bodies
Classification	igneous rock, lamprophyre
Alteration	hydrothermal alteration of olivine, pyroxene, biotite and plagioclase (if present) is common
Occurrence	normally as narrow dykes, sills, sheets and plugs, more rarely as lavas; usually associated with diorites and syenites
Examples	Sweden, Germany, Norway, the former USSR, the USA, England and Greenland

Kimberlite

Kimberlite

fragments of crystal and rock

Kimberlite

mica

garnet

Serpentinized kimberlite

Geologists now regard kimberlite, the primary source of diamonds, as a variety of lamprophyre. It was named after South Africa's Kimberley diamond mine. The term *blue ground* is used for the unoxidized, slate-blue or blue-green kimberlite that occurs below the superficial oxidized zone. Kimberlite is rare, but is of great interest because of its unusual mineralogy and because it contains rocks brought up from the Earth's mantle. They may form either when melt consolidates at depth, or they may reach the surface as fluidized fragmental kimberlite that forces its way up through a pipe-like structure, called a diatreme. Kimberlite is an important source for gem-quality pyrope crystals called *Cape ruby*.

KIMBERLITE

Colour	bluish, greenish or black
Mineralogy	olivine (serpentinized), with variable amounts of phlogopite mica, pyroxenes, carbonate and chromite, also minor amounts of e.g. garnet and rutile
Texture	variable grain size characteristic, with fairly large rock or mineral fragments in a fine-grained matrix
Structure	variable, can be a fragmental tuffaceous or agglomeratic rock, or fragmented material cemented by massive kimberlite, or as a massive rock with igneous textures e.g. flow textures
Classification	ultramafic igneous rock, a variety of lamprophyre; ultrabasic
Occurrence	forms sills, dykes and small diatremes (cylindrical or irregularly shaped bodies drilled through enclosing rocks by gas-charged magma); injected into ancient, upwarped shield areas along broad zones of weakness, also on margins of major structural blocks
Examples	South Africa, S and W USA, Brazil, Sierra Leone, Ghana and Liberia

Ignimbrite

Ignimbrite is an ash-flow tuff (see Ash and Tuff). The name comes from the Latin words meaning 'fire shower'. It consists of fragments of crystal and rock in a matrix of glass shards which are usually welded together. Ignimbrites are formed from pyroclastic flows, which geologists believe were caused by the collapse of a volcanic column of rhyolite or dacite. The flows are highly mobile and may travel 10–100 km (6–62 miles) from the volcanic vent. The particles are extremely hot and, when they come to rest, they weld together. Ignimbrites can cover up to 1000 km² (390 sq mi) in area. No large ignimbrite eruption has ever been observed. Ignimbrite is used as a building store.

Ignimbrite

pumice fragment

Ignimbrite

Ignimbrite

flattened pumice fragments

IGNIMBRITE

Composition	glass of rhyolite or dacite composition; crystals of plagioclase, sanidine (alkali feldspar) or quartz, also of pyroxene, hornblende or biotite; some rock fragments, also pumice
Structure	pumice fragments may be flattened, particularly near the base of the flow, and these are known as fiamme; may show layering or columnar jointing; individual units often very uniform over wide areas but individual units are unstratified and unsorted
Classification	pyroclastic igneous rock, of acid to intermediate composition
Alteration	may devitrify, glass shards being replaced by an intergrowth of feldspar and cristobalite (silica); more extensive devitrification may result in the development of spherulites
Occurrence	often erupt from arcuate fissures around the crest of broad, up-arched domes or caldera faults; also from linear fractures
Examples	New Mexico, Alaska and Montana (USA), Australia and Chile

Agglomerate

Agglomerates are pyroclastic rocks formed from fragments generated directly by volcanic action. These fragments may be individual crystals, or fragments of crystal, glass or rock. Agglomerates are composed of consolidated or unconsolidated coarse material in which rounded grains predominate. The composition of the fragments may range from acid to basic, according to the parent magma (lava). It may also include fragments torn from the side of the volcano. An agglomerate flow occurs when incandescent solid fragments, suspended in hot, expanding gases, rush down the slopes of the volcano, reaching speeds of more than 100 km/h (62 mph).

Volcanic bomb

Spindle-shaped volcanic bomb

Agglomerate

Agglomerate

clast of basic volcanic rock

AGGLOMERATE

Composition	individual crystals or fragments of crystal, glass or rock of variable composition
Texture	coarse-grained – greater than 64 mm (2.5 in) – predominantly rounded fragments in a finer-grained matrix; may be highly vesicular
Structure	may include rounded, ellipsoidal or spindle-shaped volcanic bombs, representing fragments of molten lava ejected from the volcano and gaining their shape on cooling in flight; bombs may have vesicular interiors, and glassy surfaces which have cracked due to sudden release of gases
Classification	pyroclastic igneous rock
Occurrence	formed during volcanic activity, accumulating within the crater, or on the flanks; associated with tuffs and lavas
Examples	Paricutín (Mexico), Vulcano and Stromboli, Lipari Islands, Etna and Vesuvius (Italy), Mont Pelée (Martinique)

Ash and Tuff

Volcanic ash is a pyroclastic rock, composed of fine grains less than 2 mm (0.01 in) in diameter. The ash exploded out of a volcano may fall through the air and settle in beds, called *ash-falls* when unconsolidated, or *ash-fall tuffs* when consolidated. The ash can vary in composition. It may be named *crystal tuff*, *vitric* (glassy) *tuff* or *lithic tuff* (mostly rock fragments). Rock fragments between 2 and 64 mm (0.01—2.5 in) in diameter formed from the ejection of molten lava are called *lapilli*. Ash-flows occur when ash mixed with hot gases is exploded out of volcanoes and flows rapidly downhill. When this material is consolidated, it is called an *ash-flow tuff*. Welded tuffs are called *welded ash-flow tuffs* or *ignimbrites*.

Lithic tuff

Crystal tuff

Tuff

ASH AND TUFF

Colour	white or grey powder when newly fallen, either alone or with pyroclastic matter
Composition	ash-fall tuffs composed of a mixture of rock fragments, crystals and glass shards; ash-flow tuffs usually glassy, of rhyolite to dacite composition, and may contain crystals of felsic minerals; rock fragments and pumice common
Texture	fine-grained – less than 2 mm (0.01 in) diameter; glass shards show cusp-shaped outlines; lapilli are usually rounded or ellipsoidal; loosely textured and porous
Structure	ash-fall tuffs often well-bedded; ash-flow tuffs unsorted and unstratified
Classification	pyroclastic igneous rock
Alteration	highly susceptible to change; rapidly weathered or altered, leading to colour differences between successive beds
Occurrence	associated with explosive volcanic activity; occurs with agglomerates and lava flows; particle size decreases away from the vent because lighter ash carried farthest by the wind
Examples	nearly all the world's well-known volcanoes

Greisen

Greisen, a coarse-grained, grey, metamorphic rock of glittering appearance, is composed mainly of quartz, pale silvery-green mica, and topaz. It is formed by a process called *greisening* (the pneumatolytic alteration of granite). This process occurs when vapours carrying boron, fluorine and lithium pass through and out of the cooling rock. The original biotite and feldspar of the parent granite are replaced by quartz, lithium-bearing mica (lepidolite or zinnwaldite), tourmaline and kaolinite. Greisen is sometimes of economic importance as a source of tin and tungsten.

Greisen with cassiterite

Greisen

Greisen with beryl

beryl

GREISEN

Colour	greyish, of glittering appearance
Mineralogy	quartz, white mica; may contain topaz, tourmaline, kaolinite, apatite, fluorite; also ore minerals, e.g. cassiterite, rutile, wolframite, chalcopyrite
Composition	parent rock granite
Texture	coarse grain-size; granular
Structure	as veins, which frequently have a fissure at their centre, filled or partly filled with quartz and ore minerals; the veins may form a well-defined pattern, or may form a closely interconnecting framework which may take over the whole granite
Classification	contact metasomatic rock
Occurrence	a pneumatolitically altered granite, forms veins up to a few tens of cm wide which pass gradually into the surrounding granite
Examples	SW England, Mourne Mountains (Ireland), Klondike district and Esmeralda County, Nevada (USA); younger granites (N Nigeria)

Geologists generally use the term skarn for contact-metamorphosed limestones (calcareous hornfels) that contain other minerals. Skarns are formed when a magma is intruded into limestone, and silicon-. iron- and magnesium-rich fluids react with the calcareous rock to give silicate minerals. Skarns may be associated with ore deposits of sulphides of copper, iron, lead and zinc. They often provide good mineral specimens. The term skarn originally referred to waste rock (gangue) from iron ores. Other rocks called skarn include regionally metamorphosed limestones. These types are not described here.

Skarn

andradite garnet

Skarn

grossular garnet

Andradite pyrite skarn

SKARN

Colour	brown, black, grey; variable on a small scale
Mineralogy	calcite associated with other minerals including ugrandite garnets, clinopyroxene, olivine, idocrase, periclase, serpentine and calcic amphibole; often forms the host rock for ore minerals such as magnetite and copper sulphides
Composition	calcareous impure with iron-rich silicates
Texture	fine- to coarse-grained, granoblastic
Structure	associated minerals are often clustered in layers, radiating masses or nodules; massive, banded or bedded
Classification	contact metamorphic, metasomatic rock
Occurrence	in the contact aureoles of a variety of plutons
Examples	Crestmore, California (USA), Scawt Hill (Ireland), Skye (Scotland), Dartmoor (England), Doubtful Sound (New Zealand), Oslo (Norway)

Spotted slate

As its name implies, spotted slate has the texture and structure of slate, but with a spotted appearance. Spotted slates are altered slates, which are usually found alongside unaltered slates. They occur on the outer parts of contact aureoles. They represent low-grade contact metamorphism, just as slate represents the low-grade regional metamorphism of such rocks as shales. Towards the igneous intrusion, the spots become recognizable as ovoid porphyroblasts of cordierite or prismatic crystals of chiastolite, a variety of andalusite. The grains start to recrystallize and any relict slaty cleavage becomes indistinct. The spotted or porphyroblastic rocks then pass into hornfelses of a higher grade adjacent to the intrusion.

Spotted slate

Spotted slate

Spotted slate

SPOTTED SLATE

Colour	black, purple, grey-green to grey with darker spots
Mineralogy	often too fine-grained for identification by the naked eye; spots are of andalusite and cordierite
Composition	pelitic
Texture	fine-grained
Structure	pre-existing slaty cleavage may be lost and rock becomes more massive; may preserve relict sedimentary bedding and original sedimentary structures such as channels and ripple marks
Classification	low-grade contact metamorphic rock
Occurrence	on the outer regions of contact aureoles in pelitic rocks; associated with slates unaffected by the contact aureole and hornfelses nearer to the intrusion
Examples	Bar-Andlau, Vosges (France), Orijarvi (Finland), Sierra Nevada, California (USA), Aberfoyle slate, Perthshire (Scotland), the Coniston Flags and Skiddaw Slate, Lake District (England)

Hornfels

Hornfelses are hard, fine- to medium-grained, metamorphic rocks, often of a flinty appearance. These baked rocks, formed in the innermost parts of contact aureoles, contain minerals characteristic of high temperatures and low pressures. Some hornfelses are named after the rocks from which they are derived, such as pelitic-, calcareous-, quartzofeldspathic-, and basic hornfelses. Some are named by porphyroblasts present, such as andalusite-, cordierite- and pyroxene-hornfelses. Andalusite porphyroblasts may contain inclusions. In the variety *chiastolite*, the inclusions form a cross-shape. Small igneous intrusions may produce a narrow band of hornfels called a 'baked contact'. Rapid cooling of the magma produces a 'chilled margin' in contact with the hornfels.

Hornfels

HORNFELS

Colour	very varied depending on type of source rock
Mineralogy	very varied, depending on source rock and temperature of heating; andalusite or sillimanite may be present, never kyanite; calcite in calcareous rocks, not aragonite; cordierite and pyroxene are common
Composition	varied, can be any rock
Texture	approximately equidimensional grains typically less than 1 mm (0.04 in); porphyroblasts or phenocrysts may be present; contact metamorphism drastically reduces or eradicates such structures as schistosity
Structure	medium- to large-scale structures of country rock are preserved
Classification	medium- to high-grade, contact metamorphic rock
Occurrence	hornfelses occur in aureoles near to the igneous intrusion and in xenoliths; also near, and grading into, slates and spotted slates; common near granite batholiths
Examples	Scotland, Ireland, South Africa, Newfoundland, Tasmania

Spotted hornfels

Hornfels

Marble

Marble is, strictly, a crystalline carbonate rock formed by the metamorphism of limestone. It is much softer than quartzite and is easily scratched with a knife. Calcite marbles effervesce with dilute hydrochloric acid. A famous source of the white marble used for statues is Carrara, Italy. Ophicalcite is a variegated green and white variety, containing forsterite and/or diopside. Marble is much used in buildings. The Taj Mahal, in Agra, India, is constructed of white calcite marble. Commercially, the term marble includes other rocks and minerals, including alabaster.

Marble

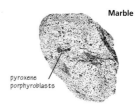

pyroxene porphyroblasts

Ophicalcite

Marble

MARBLE

Colour	may be uniformly white and glistening, light brown or grey; also variegated with green, red or black
Mineralogy	95 per cent calcite and/or dolomite; silicate minerals, such as wollastonite, diopside or forsterite may form from siliceous limestones; many other minerals may be formed depending on impurities in the limestone
Composition	calcareous
Texture	medium- to coarse-grained; pure calcite marbles recrystallize towards a granoblastic texture with increasing grade; may show saccharoidal texture
Structure	often massive, but may preserve sedimentary structures such as bedding; fossils may be preserved at low grades only; sometimes folded
Classification	regional (greenschist, amphibolite or granulite facies) or contact metamorphism
Occurrence	in most regional metamorphic terrains, also in contact aureoles
Examples	Italy, C India; also Skye (Scotland)

Folded quartzite

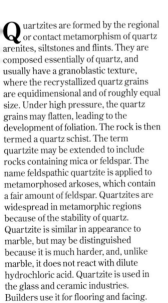

mica-rich layers

Quartzite with chalcopyrite

chalcopyrite

Quartzites are formed by the regional or contact metamorphism of quartz arenites, siltstones and flints. They are composed essentially of quartz, and usually have a granoblastic texture, where the recrystallized quartz grains are equidimensional and of roughly equal size. Under high pressure, the quartz grains may flatten, leading to the development of foliation. The rock is then termed a quartz schist. The term quartzite may be extended to include rocks containing mica or feldspar. The name feldspathic quartzite is applied to metamorphosed arkoses, which contain a fair amount of feldspar. Quartzites are widespread in metamorphic regions because of the stability of quartz. Quartzite is similar in appearance to marble, but may be distinguished because it is much harder, and, unlike marble, it does not react with dilute hydrochloric acid. Quartzite is used in the glass and ceramic industries. Builders use it for flooring and facing.

QUARTZITE

Colour	white, grey or reddish
Mineralogy	mostly quartz, may contain some feldspar or mica
Composition	siliceous
Texture	medium-grained, granoblastic
Structure	generally massive, but may sometimes show sedimentary structures, such as bedding or cross-bedding; may show foliation and folding where microscopic layers of mica alternate with layers of quartz
Classification	regional or contact metamorphism of sandstone
Occurrence	in regional metamorphic terrains; derived from mature sorted sediments and conglomerates and found associated with other metasediments, such as marble, phyllite or schist
Examples	Scottish Highlands, County Galway (Ireland), Deccan (India), Guyana, Venezuela

Slate

Slate is formed from the low-temperature regional metamorphism of fine-grained shales or mudstones. Its chief characteristic is that it easily splits along roughly parallel surfaces, known as *cleavage planes*. These are caused by the alignment of flat mineral crystals, especially micas, during the deformation and compression episodes which turned the original rock into a slate. As slate is a relatively low-grade rock, the aligned crystals are small and the cleavage planes are closely-spaced. Deformation under higher pressures and temperatures produces rocks which contain larger aligned crystals, such as phyllites and schists. Because of its cleavage planes, slate splits into parallel-sided slabs, a property that makes it an important roofing material. Some slates have more than one cleavage direction. The remnants of original sedimentary features, such as graded bedding, may be visible either parallel or slightly inclined to the cleavage. Distorted fossils are found occasionally in slate.

Slate containing iron pyrites

SLATE

Colour	mostly grey to black (graphite); may be purple or red (hematite), or green (chlorite)
Mineralogy	chlorite, micas, graphite, quartz; pyrite may occur in relatively large crystals, due to the reduction of iron in the presence of organic matter
Composition	pelitic
Texture	fine-grained, grains too small to distinguish with the naked eye
Structure	slaty cleavage; look for pale green, ovoid reduction spots; rarely original sedimentary structures and distorted fossils
Classification	regional metamorphism of greenschist facies
Occurrence	widespread in regional metamorphic terrains; may be interlayered with metamorphosed greywackes and volcanic rocks
Examples	Skiddaw (England), Aar Massif, Alps

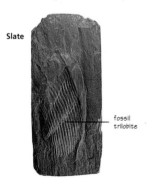

Slate

fossil trilobite

crenulations

Phyllite

Graphitic phyllite

The grey or green rock phyllite is formed from the regional metamorphism of clays or shales. It is intermediate in grain size between slate and schist. Phyllite is distinguished from slate by the sheen on the cleavage surface. It is distinguished from schist, because the constituent grains in phyllite are too small to see with the naked eye. The cleavage is well-developed and phyllite splits easily into slabs. The cleavage is caused by the almost perfect parallel alignment of the grains. In phyllites, unlike slates, the fabric is often undulatory, caused by superimposed folds or crenulations. A similar rock, phyllonite, is produced by the retrograde metamorphism of higher grade rocks such as schists. The name phyllite comes from the Greek *phyllos*, meaning 'leaf'.

Chlorite phyllite

PHYLLITE

Colour	green grey to dark grey
Mineralogy	muscovite, chlorite and quartz; minor constituents are magnetite or pyrite, feldspar and sometimes biotite
Composition	pelitic
Texture	fine-grained, the individual grains too small to identify with the naked eye; may show porphyroblastic texture, with porphyroblasts of albite or manganese-rich garnet
Structure	shows a well-developed cleavage, the surfaces showing a lustrous sheen; commonly shows one or more sets of crenulations (microfolds) and lineations
Classification	regional metamorphism of greenschist facies
Occurrence	in regional metamorphic terrains, forming part of a progressive series slate-phyllite-mica schist with increasing metamorphic grade; associated with other metamorphosed sediments of the greenschist facies
Examples	found in Eastern and Central Alps, Scotland, Norway, Australia, USA, Germany and Belgium

Mica schist

Mica schist is a medium- to coarse-grained rock formed by the regional metamorphism of pelitic rocks. It is characterized by the parallel arrangement of the constituent minerals. This gives it a marked foliation known as *schistosity*. Many rocks possessing this foliation are called schists, but most are mica-rich and formed from pelitic sediments, such as clays, mudstones and shales. They are named after the prominent minerals within them. With increasing temperature, the minerals within a schist gradually change. This is especially noticeable with the porphyroblasts. In a classic terrain in the Scottish Highlands, these appear in the order biotite, garnet, staurolite, kyanite and sillimanite.

Garnet mica schist

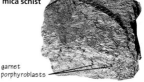

garnet porphyroblasts

Quartz biotite schist

schistosity

kyanite porphyroblast

Kyanite biotite schist

MICA SCHIST

Colour	greyish and sparkling, white grains of quartz may be visible; colour of porphyroblasts variable
Mineralogy	muscovite and biotite micas, quartz, feldspar and chlorite; may contain porphyroblasts of andalusite, biotite, garnet, staurolite, kyanite or sillimanite if pelitic, or hornblende or actinolite if marly
Composition	pelitic
Texture	medium or coarse-grained; commonly porphyroblastic; porphyroblasts may show an alignment of hornblende needles or arrangement into a wheat-sheaf pattern; garnets may form in layers
Structure	characterized by well-developed schistosity, which may be folded one or more times, and may also show lineations
Classification	regional metamorphism of greenschist or amphibolite facies
Occurrence	widespread in metamorphic terrains, may be associated with other metasediments
Examples	Norway, Scotland, the Alps, USA, New Zealand, Japan

Gneiss

Augen gneiss

Streaky gneiss

Banded gneiss

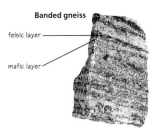

felsic layer

mafic layer

GNEISS

Colour	commonly formed of alternating dark and light (white, pink or grey) bands
Mineralogy	quartz and feldspar, may also contain biotite and/or hornblende, also various porphyroblasts, such as garnet, staurolite, sillimanite or cordierite
Composition	varied, may be igneous or sedimentary
Texture	medium- to coarse-grained, usually coarser than schists; bands and lenses of alternating granular and flaky minerals, less than 50 per cent crystals showing parallel orientation; may show augen crystals
Structure	bands and foliations may be folded one or more times; shows other structures, such as waves, streaks and veins
Classification	regional metamorphism of amphibolite or granulite facies
Occurrence	distributed in regional metamorphic terrains
Examples	Precambrian shield regions of Scandinavia, Canada, Brazil, Australia; pelitic gneisses in France and Germany; granitic gneiss in the Alps

Gneiss is a foliated rock formed during regional metamorphism. It consists of alternating dark and light bands. The thickness of the bands varies from about 0.5 mm (0.02 in) for the dark layers and up to 40 cm (16 in) or more for the light layers. Many gneisses are quartzo-feldspathic. These are formed from such rocks as arkosic (feldspar-rich) sediments, acid volcanic rocks or granitic rocks. Varieties are distinguished by characteristic minerals (e.g. staurolite gneiss), texture (e.g. augen gneiss), structure (e.g. pencil gneiss), or the parent rock (e.g. granitic gneiss). Gneisses often represent the highest-grade metamorphic rock in an area. They may be associated with, and grade into schists and migmatites.

Migmatites

Migmatite

- paleosome
- neosome
- biotite-rich layer

Migmatite

Migmatite

M igmatites are complex rocks formed at high temperatures, comprising a dark, schist-like or gneissose component (*paleosome*) and a light-coloured granitic component (*neosome*). Most geologists agree that they represent stages in the formation of granite magmas by partial melting of the existing rock. The variety *agmatite* consists of angular blocks of paleosome surrounded by veins of neosome, resembling breccia. In *nebulite* ('cloudy' migmatite), the components grade into each other, giving a diffuse appearance. The *ptygmatic veins* that occur in some migmatites are small, intensely folded veins of neosome. Migmatites are used as a building stone and occasionally as polished slabs for decorative use.

MIGMATITES

Colour	a mixture of a dark coloured component (also called host rock) and a white, pink or grey granitic component
Mineralogy	host rock minerals are the same as for schists and gneisses of high metamorphic grade; essential granitic minerals are quartz and alkali feldspar
Composition	usually felsic or intermediate
Texture	medium- to coarse-grained components may have the texture of schists or gneisses, including augen structures
Classification	high grade metamorphism
Occurrence	often found in old Archaean rocks in continental shield areas (old stable areas which have not been subjected to major tectonic action) where deep erosion has revealed rocks formed at depth; also in smaller bodies in contact aureoles close to large granite intrusions
Examples	common in Finland, Canada, Massif Central (France), Scottish Highlands

Amphibolites are usually formed by the metamorphism of basic igneous rocks, namely basaltic tuffs, lava, or intrusive dolerite. But some are also derived from marls (calcium-rich pelitic rocks). They are formed under conditions of medium temperature, that is around 600°–750°C (1100°–1380°F). The closely related rock epidote amphibolite contains epidote, albite and hornblende. It forms from the same kinds of rocks, but at slightly lower temperatures. Hornblende granulite is formed at higher temperatures. It contains orthopyroxene as well as hornblende and plagioclase.

Amphibolite

Schistose amphibolite

schistosity

Garnet amphibolite

AMPHIBOLITE

Colour	green to dark green or black; often speckled or striped with white or grey
Mineralogy	hornblende (or occasionally actinolite or tremolite) and plagioclase; minor amounts of quartz, garnet, biotite, diopside cummingtonite
Composition	mafic or calc-pelitic
Texture	may be massive, medium-grained, equigranular rocks or foliated (*hornblende schists*) or lineated; may show dark and light bands, the individual stripes being 1 mm–2 cm (0.04–0.8 in) thick; relict igneous textures and structures are sometimes preserved; may occasionally contain porphyroblasts of garnet
Structure	often forms disrupted lenses and fragments within schists
Classification	regional metamorphic rock of amphibolite facies
Occurrence	widely distributed in old shield areas and younger orogenic belts; often associated with garnet-, kyanite-, staurolite- or sillimanite-bearing schists and gneisses
Examples	USA, Australia, Scotland, Ireland, Greenland

Glaucophane schist

Glaucophane schist

Glaucophane schist

Glaucophane schist

garnet porphyroblast

G laucophane schists are rocks with a characteristic blue colour, hence their alternative name, blueschists. They occur in regions where rocks have been deeply buried but at relatively low temperatures. This situation occurs along subduction zones, where cold, mostly mafic ocean crust is pulled down as a slab along destructive plate margins. Associated rocks include eclogites and so-called ophiolitic debris, containing shales and greywackes formed on the ocean floor. Blueschists do not occur in Precambrian rocks. Some geologists have argued that this fact demonstrates that plate tectonic processes did not operate in the Precambrian.

GLAUCOPHANE SCHIST

Colour	dark blue or purple
Mineralogy	abundant glaucophane (a blue amphibole) with quartz, albite, jadeite, garnet or chlorite
Composition	mafic
Texture	fine- to medium-grained; poorly schistose with alignment of glaucophane needles
Structure	shows chaotic relationships in the field, forming broken blocks along with ophiolite fragments in a sheared matrix of shale, greywacke or serpentinite; may contain lenses of eclogite
Classification	high pressure, low temperature regional metamorphism
Occurrence	uncommon; mainly in orogenic mountain building belts such as the Alps/Himalayas and the circum-Pacific region
Examples	Channel Islands, Ballantrae (Scotland), Anglesey (Wales), Coastal Range, California (USA), Svalbard (Norway), Sanbagawa and Sangun (Japan); Western Alps, New Caledonia (Canada)

Eclogite is an attractive rock containing green omphacite and red garnet. It often has a banded structure and may contain large porphyroblasts. Eclogite has the same chemical composition as basalt, but its specific gravity is about 3.5 as compared with 3.0 for basalt. Its higher density reflects its formation at high pressures and at great depths. There are three groups of eclogites. Common eclogites (Group C) are probably metamorphosed dolerite dykes or sills, or basalt lava. Magnesium-rich garnet pyroxenites (Group G) originate in the upper mantle. Some geologists consider them to be igneous rocks. Iron- and sodium-rich ophiolitic eclogites (Group O) were formed when oceanic crust was deeply buried by subduction.

Eclogite

Eclogite

garnet

pyroxene

Eclogite

ECLOGITE

Colour	red and green
Mineralogy	essential minerals are garnet and the aluminium-containing clinopyroxene omphacite; accessory minerals include hornblende, zoisite, quartz, kyanite, mica, rutile, olivine, glaucophane, epidote and dolomite, but never plagioclase
Composition	mafic
Texture	medium- to coarse-grained; often large garnet or pyroxene porphyroblasts
Classification	high pressure, low-, medium- or high-temperature regional metamorphism
Structure	often massive and banded
Occurrence	common eclogites as small bodies in migmatites or gneisses; garnet pyroxenites as nodules and lenses in kimberlites, basic lavas and ultramafic rocks; ophiolitic eclogites as intercalations and lenses in blueschists
Examples	Group C: Germany, Austria, Scotland and Norway; Group G: Bohemian Massif, Norway, South Africa and Hawaii; Group O: USA, Italy and Switzerland

Serpentinite

Serpentinite

Garnet serpentinite

Serpentinite is a soft, compact metamorphic rock composed of serpentine minerals. It is formed by the hydrous alteration (alteration through the addition of water) of olivines and pyroxenes in ultramafic rocks. Some relict (unaltered) rocks may remain. Attractive varieties are used for ornaments and facing stones. The Inuits of North America and the Lapps of northern Europe have used soapstones and serpentinites for artefacts. It is also used as a source of asbestos, chromite (for chromium), refractories, and talc (for paper making).

Serpentinite with stichtite

stichtite

SERPENTINITE

Colour	pale green to greenish black, often with red or bright green streaks or blotches; weathered surfaces are yellow-orange to red-brown
Mineralogy	wholly or mainly serpentine minerals antigorite, chrysotile or lizardite; may contain minor amounts of olivine, pyroxene and spine and also minerals such as talc, chlorite and iron oxides
Composition	ultramafic
Texture	medium- to coarse-grained; compact; has a smooth to splintery fracture
Structure	may be massive, with relics of ultramafic parent rock, or sheared, showing many polished slip surfaces cut by intercrossing veins of fibrous chrysotile (asbestos)
Classification	low-temperature, low pressure, hydrous alteration product
Occurrence	stocks, dykes and lenses, often grading into peridotite
Examples	England, Alps, USA, Canada, Cuba, New Zealand, Norway, the former Yugoslavia, the Himalayas, Cuba, Phillipines, Albania, Cyprus

Mylonite

Mylonite is a cataclastic rock formed during dynamic metamorphism. The term *cataclasis* comes from the Greek words meaning 'breaking down'. Mylonite is formed where rocks react by ductile flow, whereas *fault breccia* is formed where rocks react by breaking. In mylonite, the grain size gradually decreases as the rock is strained, but it increases as the rock starts to recover. The rock being deformed can be of any kind. As it is ground up, the original fragments form a smaller and smaller proportion of the whole rock. Unlike fault breccia, mylonite is always a cohesive rock.

Mylonite

Mylonite

Mylonite

feldspar porphyroclast

MYLONITE

Composition	variable
Texture	complex; strained porphyroclasts (relict crystals) are set in a finer-grained matrix formed by the crushing of minerals of different physical properties; fragments of original rock (protolith) may form more than 50 per cent of the rock ('protomylonite'), 10–50 per cent ('ultramylonite') or less than 10 per cent (mylonite); porphyroclasts may be lozenge-shaped, forming an augen rock, or may be reduced to a fine-grained aggregate which is streaked out as a 'flaser' structure to give a layered or banded structure
Classification	dynamic metamorphic rock
Occurrence	forms at depth in zones of shearing, almost invariably occurring in regional metamorphic gneisses or granulites at the margins of orogenic belts; belts of mylonites and other cataclastic rocks are belts, are commonly vertical, and often many kilometres wide
Examples	San Andreas Fault (USA), Insubric Line (Alps)

Conglomerates

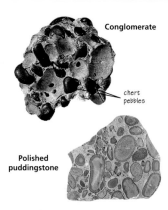

Conglomerate

chert pebbles

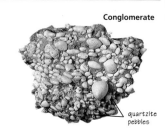

Conglomerate

quartzite pebbles

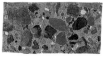

Polished puddingstone

Polished conglomerate

CONGLOMERATES

Colour	variable and dependent on type and proportion of pebbles
Mineralogy	pebbles very varied in composition; variable proportions of sand or silt matrix which may be cemented to a greater or lesser extent by calcite or silica
Texture	coarse-grained mixture of two main components, one fine- to medium-grained, the other rounded fragments of pebble to boulder size
Structure	little internal structure; fossils rare
Occurrence	often found above unconformities and associated with sandstones and arkoses
Examples	puddingstone in Hertfordshire (England) and Lucerne (Switzerland), the Precambrian Ingleton Series of N England, Triassic conglomerates of eastern USA, gold-bearing conglomerates of Witwatersrand (South Africa); modern gravels are ubiquitous in river beds and beaches

Conglomerates are *rudaceous* (coarse-grained) rocks composed of rounded fragments set in a mass of fine- to medium-sized grains (the *matrix*). The rounded fragments range in size from pebbles to boulders. They may consist of almost any hard rock, especially such weather-resistant types as chert or quartzite. Deposited from fast-moving water, conglomerates form on beaches and river beds. They are often formed during marine transgressions – that is, when the sea floods a large area relatively rapidly. Hence, conglomerates often occur above unconformities. They can mark the bottom of a new sequence of rocks and form a major geological boundary.

B reccias, like conglomerates, are coarse-grained rocks. They differ from conglomerates in that the large fragments set in the fine- to medium-grained matrix are angular and unworn. Because large and heavy fragments are much more easily rounded by erosion during transport than smaller grains, the angular fragments must not been moved far from the source rock. The angular fragments in some breccias are formed by landslides or the heaps of scree (talus) at the foot of steep slopes. Others are formed when limestone caves collapse. Fault breccia is produced by the fragmentation of rocks during fault movements.

Breccia

Fault Breccia

Breccia

BRECCIAS

Colour	variable
Mineralogy	rock fragments may be of any rock type; variable proportions of sand or silt matrix, often cemented by calcite or silica
Texture	coarse-grained mixture of two components, one of fine- to medium-size grains, the other of angular fragments of pebble to boulder size
Occurrence	often occur above unconformities and associated with conglomerate, arkose or sandstone; may occur close to a fault zone
Examples	the 310 m (1020 ft) thick Cow Head Breccia of Newfoundland (Canada) is especially spectacular; it is found in dolomites and limestones of Beekmantown, Pennsylvania and Siyeh Mountains (USA), Cotham marble, Bristol (England) and Eilean Dubh dolomite, Sutherland (Scotland)

Till and Tillites

Till, also called *boulder clay*, is the unconsolidated matter deposited by glaciers and ice sheets from the Pleistocene glaciation. The consolidated form is called *tillite*. Tillites are older rocks from the four other major glaciations. Till is characterized by a wide range of particle sizes and types of fragments, the largest boulders weighing several tonnes. The material was originally gathered up by moving bodies of ice, transported, and finally dumped when the ice melted. This is an example of erosion where the material is transported with virtually no sorting or grading. Till and tillite are important indicators of glaciation and possibly of a major Ice Age in Earth history.

Tillite

clast

Tillite

granitic boulder

fine-grained matrix

Tillite

rock fragment

TILL AND TILLITES

Colour	tills are red-brown to grey and when consolidated to tillites are dark grey to greenish black
Mineralogy	rocks of sedimentary, igneous or metamorphic origin set in a matrix of clay and/or sand-grade material
Texture	fine to very large grain size; angular to rounded pebbles, cobbles and boulders in finer matrix
Structure	no bedding or internal structures
Occurrence	glaciated terrains of any rock type
Examples	boulder clays formed during the Ice Age in the Pleistocene epoch are found in N Germany and Britain (e.g. the Yorkshire coast), and in Canada and the N USA; older tillites include the Dwyka Tillite of South Africa, the Talchir Boulder Bed of India and the Huronian tillites of Canada; modern boulder clays are forming in Greenland, Spitzbergen and Antarctica

Sandstones: Quartz arenites

Desert sandstone

Quartz arenite

Quartz arenite

bedding disturbed by burrows

Orthoquartzite

bedding

Q uartz arenites. or orthoquartzites, are *arenaceous* (medium-grained) sandstones containing a high proportion of quartz. Some were deposited in water, usually in shallow marine environments, while others, termed *aeolian*, were wind-blown sands deposited in desert environments. Porous sandstones are important as aquifers for ground water and as reservoirs for oil and natural gas. Well-cemented sandstones are used in building. Finer-quality sands are used in glass manufacture. Where little high-quality brick clay is available, as in Germany, silica sand is used in calcium silicate bricks. *Ganister* is a quartz arenite with good refractory properties used to line furnaces.

SANDSTONES

Colour	varies, often white or pale grey when derived from shallow water, such as a beach; red when of desert origin; in greensands, the colour is due to precipitation of glauconite
Mineralogy	over 95 per cent quartz grains; varying amounts of matrix and cement affect porosity and strength
Texture	medium-grained; mostly well-sorted and rounded; wind-blown grains are well-rounded with a frosted surface
Structure	bedding in marine sandstones is usually easily seen and sedimentary structures, e.g. cross-stratification and graded bedding, are common, as are a variety of fossils and concretions; in aeolian sandstones, large scale cross-bedding (dune-bedding) is often seen
Occurrence	ubiquitous; found in association with most sedimentary rock types
Examples	quartzites of N Wales, Shropshire (England), NW Scotland and France; Lower Cretaceous greensands common in N America

Sandstones: Lithic arenites

Quartz makes up a much lower proportion of the grains in lithic arenites than in quartz arenites, though it is still the main component. Besides quartz, lithic arenites contain a variety of other mineral fragments, that can be derived from any rock that can give sand-sized particles. However, feldspar grains form a relatively minor component. Lithic arenites, or *litharenites*, are a major rock group. They comprise a high proportion of the sandstones found around the world. They are formed in rivers, deltas, shallow seas and sea basins.

Lithic arenite

Polished slab

Lithic arenite

SANDSTONES

Colour	variable
Mineralogy	wide variety of rock fragments with up to about 75 per cent quartz grains; less than 15 per cent fine-grained material
Texture	medium-grained; may range widely in degrees of sorting and angularity of grains
Structure	bedding is often apparent as are sedimentary structures; fossils and various concretions may be present
Occurrence	found in association with most other sedimentary rock types relatively close to source of lithic grains
Examples	found among many sandstones of all ages; Old Red Sandstone-age rock of the Welsh borderland (Britain), Palaeocene rocks of Dakota (USA), Permian rocks of India and Australia, and Tertiary rocks of the northern Mediterranean

Arkoses are feldspar-rich sandstones that are derived from granitic rocks and gneisses. The feldspar is mostly alkali feldspar, usually microcline. Arkoses contain little fine-grained matrix material and the feldspar grains are angular. This often gives the rocks a gritty appearance and feel. Because feldspars weather to clay minerals, arkoses generally form in relatively dry or cold climates. In humid environments, their formation depends on rapid burial and removal from circulating water. The red or pink colour is usually derived from the feldspar, but some hematite may also be present.

Arkose

Coarse-grained arkose

Arkose

SANDSTONES

Colour	grey, pink, or red
Mineralogy	contains more than 25 per cent feldspar and usually up to 50 per cent; the remainder is often quartz with some biotite and muscovite; calcite or iron oxide cement
Texture	medium-grained, usually at the coarsest end of the range, with up to 15 per cent of a fine-grained matrix; grains are angular
Structure	bedding may be well developed or obscure; cross-lamination and cross-bedding is common
Occurrence	formed by the degradation of granites and granite gneisses, followed by transport over only short distances and deposition in rivers, lakes or shallow seas; arkoses often occur above unconformities near to granitic rocks and are associated with granite-derived conglomerate
Examples	Torridon sandstone (Scotland), Vosges Mountains (France), Black Forest, (Germany), sandstones of the Californian Coastal Range (USA), and sandstones of Millstone Grit (N England)

Sandstones: Greywackes

Greywackes are typically dark, hard rocks formed by turbidity currents. These currents occur when a mass of sediment at the top of a continental slope (the edge of a continental shelf) is set in motion, perhaps by an earthquake. The sediment, forming a dense solid-liquid mixture, slumps rapidly down the slope. It is dumped at the bottom, giving rise to a formation containing greywackes. The nature and speed of turbidity currents was recognized only 20 years after one such underwater avalanche broke 12 submarine cables to the east of Newfoundland in 1929. Greywackes are usually well cemented rocks, as the sediments are rapidly buried and often subjected to mild metamorphism and tectonic processes.

Greywacke

Greywacke

carbonaceous silt pebbles

Calcareous greywacke

SANDSTONES

Colour	usually dark, from grey to black, sometimes greenish
Mineralogy	grains of quartz, feldspar and rock fragments; the fine-grained matrix cannot be distinguished by the naked eye; chlorite may impart a green colour
Texture	medium-grained; usually poorly sorted, angular grains set in a fine-grained matrix which comprises at least 15 per cent of the rock
Structure	often massive, with graded bedding common; beds are coarse-grained at the bottom and grade through to silt or clay at the top; fossils very rare; commonly have slump structures
Occurrence	formed typically in rapidly subsiding marine basins by turbidity currents, often off continental margins and in association with volcanics
Examples	in the Lower Palaeozoic rocks of Wales, Ireland and the Southern Uplands of Scotland; the Devonian-Carboniferous rocks of SW England and Germany; the Mesozoic rocks of California, Washington and Alaska (USA); and the Tertiary Waitemata Group of N New Zealand

Red siltstone

Green siltstone

Leached siltstone

Siltstones are composed of silt grains. They are intermediate in grade between sandstones and shales. The gritty feel when ground between the teeth distinguishes them from shales. Some grains in siltstones may be visible to the naked eye, especially shiny mica, quartz and feldspar crystals. Silt is a well-known deposit in lakes and slow-flowing rivers. It also occurs in large quantities in seas not too close to the shore and, in lesser amounts, in glacial deposits. Bedding is often more clearly visible than in shales, and may bear more relationship to that found in finer-grained sandstones. Ripples can give rise to some cross-stratification. Like other mudrocks, siltstones may contain nodules formed by cementing minerals such as calcite, pyrite and chert. Fossils are often abundant in siltstones.

SILTSTONES

Colour	shades of grey to black and brown to pale brown or yellow
Mineralogy	coarser grains of quartz, micas and feldspars set in a very fine-grained matrix including clay minerals; some concretions of other minerals may be present
Texture	fine-grained, with grain sizes between 0.004 and 0.06 mm (0.0002–0.002 in); grittiness by feel or by grinding softer specimens between the teeth distinguish siltstones from shales
Structure	fine bedding is common; also small-scale sedimentary structures, such as ripple marks
Occurrence	can occur in many sedimentary sequences throughout the world, often found alongside shales and sandstones
Examples	late Precambrian rock of Islay and the Caithness (Scotland), Devonian portage group in New York and most modern sediments of the Mississippi Delta (USA), the Hasawnah formation and at Wadi Ash Shati (Libya)

Clays, Shales and Mudstones

The finest grained detrital rocks are soft, plastic clays which occur only in young formations. The particles are invisible to the naked eye and clay feels smooth when worked. Shales are finely laminated or bedded rocks that split into fine layers, whereas mudstones are quite massive and well-consolidated. Clays accumulate in the deepest parts of lakes and seas where the gentlest water movements can transport the smallest particles. Fossils are often abundant. These rocks are often coloured black by carbonaceous material, or red by oxides of iron. Greenish hues are also common. Together with siltstones, these rocks are termed mudrocks.

Shale

Lime mudstone

bedding

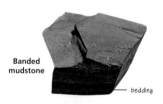

Banded mudstone

bedding

Carbonaceous shale

CLAYS, SHALES AND MUDSTONES

Colour black through grey to off-white, browns, reds and dark blues/greens

Mineralogy mainly clay minerals and detrital quartz, feldspar and micas; none can be seen by the naked eye

Texture very fine grain size – less than 0.004 mm (0.0002 in); very smooth to the touch, shales may be worked between the teeth without a gritty feel

Structure fine bedding in shales; may show sun-cracks, rain-prints and various marks left by organisms on mud flats

Occurrence often occur in association with limestones and sandstones as part of repeating cycles, reflecting marine transgressions and regressions with near-shore, shallow and deep water environments

Examples ubiquitous; also the black shales of the Lower Palaeozoic of England, Wales and Germany; the Precambrian Nonesuch Shale of Michigan (USA) is copper-bearing; the fossil-rich Burgess Shales (Australia)

Loess consists of fine detrital material that has been transported and deposited by winds. It is also known as Aeolian clay after *Aiolos*, the Greek god of the winds. It differs from muds and clays deposited in water, because it contains few or no clay minerals. Instead, it consists of extremely small, angular fragments of rock-forming minerals, especially quartz. They appear originally to have come from glacial outwash or from deserts. Loess can form high cliffs, often revealing vertical tubes with calcite linings. It is often unstratified and unconsolidated. Deposits in China and Europe can be quite thick but are remarkably uniform throughout. Loess is easily washed out and reworked by the action of water. Thus it is uncommon to find loessic rocks formed before Pleistocene times. However, one recently discovered example is from Late Precambrian rocks in northern Scandinavia. *Adobe*, a similar calcareous deposit, occurs in the Mississippi valley in the USA.

Compact loess

Poorly consolidated loess deposit

LOESS

Colour	yellow, brown, buff and grey
Mineralogy	rock-forming minerals, too small to be seen by the naked eye
Texture	very fine-grained; earthy and porous; easily crumbles to the touch
Structure	poor or no bedding apparent; few fossils
Occurrence	loess is formed from minute wind-blown particles of probable glacial origin; the rocks associated with it are thus very varied and unhelpful for identification purposes
Examples	large late Pleistocene deposits of great thickness in China, the Mississippi valley area (USA), central Europe and eastern South America; the 'loessite' of late Precambrian rocks of N Norway is one of the few positively identified pre-Pleistocene loess deposits

Fossiliferous limestones

Fossiliferous limestones consist of a large number of fossils held together mainly by a calcite cement. Biohermal limestones, formed from colonies of algae or coral and the animals living in them, are formed in shallow water, as also are biostromal limestones formed from beds made up of the shells of bottom-living organisms. Pelagic limestones, formed in deep water, consist of the skeletons of floating organisms, usually plankton. Occasionally, fossiliferous limestones form in fresh water. The types may be distinguished by the nature of the fossils they contain.

Shelly limestone

Shelly limestone

Shelly limestone

FOSSILIFEROUS LIMESTONES

Colour	variable; white, grey or cream to red, brown or black
Mineralogy	finely divided calcite mud containing larger crystals from animal skeletons; also varying amounts of chert, silt or mud
Texture	variable; from fine-grained compact, porcelain-like to very coarse; texture depends on the number and type of fossils present
Structure	bedding often apparent; the fossils may be complete or fragmented; in reef limestones the stucture of the reef may be preserved; often cut by veins of calcite
Other tests	effervesces with dilute hydrochloric acid
Occurrence	widely distributed, mainly as three types: biohermal, biostromal and pelagic limestones
Examples	biohermal include some Carboniferous limestones in England and the Great Barrier Reef (Australia); biostromal types include Purbeck Marble in England, SW Ohio (USA), Austria and modern deposits in Florida; pelagic types include Eocene limestones of the Nile valley (Egypt)

Oolitic and Pisolitic limestones

Oolitic limestone

oncoids

Pisolitic limestone

Oolitic limestone

Oolitic limestones are carbonate rocks made up mostly of ooliths (or *ooids*). They often resemble fish roe. Ooliths are formed by the precipitation of carbonate in concentric layers around a central nucleus, such as a shell fragment or a quartz grain. Pisoliths are larger grains that appear to have formed under different conditions from ooliths. A related particle, an *oncoid*, superficially resembles an oolith, but it is of algal origin. Ooliths are being formed today in the Gulf, the Red Sea, the shallow waters near the Bahamas, and the Great Salt Lake of Utah in the USA. Pisoliths occur in the coastal plans around the Gulf.

OOLITIC AND PISOLITIC LIMESTONES

Colour	white through yellow to browns and reds
Mineralogy	usually calcite ooliths in varying amounts of a finer-grained calcite matrix, but ooliths of dolomite, hematite and silica occur; some detrital quartz or clays may be present
Texture	spheres or oval shapes having a concentrically zoned inner structure, possibly dispersed, in a fine-grained matrix; ooliths are up to 1 mm (0.04 in) in diameter; pisoliths are between 2 and 10 mm (0.08–0.4 in) in diameter
Other tests	effervesces with dilute hydrochloric acid
Structure	often current bedded; varying amounts of fossil fragments
Occurrence	in warm, shallow, strongly agitated seas
Examples	Middle Jurassic Great Oolite (S England); oolitic sands are found around the Red Sea and the Gulf; pisoliths occur in sabkha zones (coastal plains) around the Gulf

Chalks

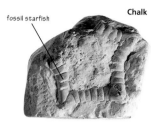

fossil starfish

Chalk

Chalk

Chalk, a pure form of limestone, is usually found in thick beds. Most chalks were formed during the Cretaceous period. This period – from 140 to 65 million years ago – was named from *creta*, the Latin word for 'chalk'. This was because high sea levels gave rise to the large areas of shallow sea needed for chalk deposition. Some chalks have layers just a few centimetres thick which have been more thoroughly cemented. Such *hardgrounds* were formed during periods of low depositon. The porous chalks of Western Europe are important as aquifers. But other well-cemented chalks are much denser and, hence, much less porous. The main constituents of chalk are the calcareous remains of micro-organisms called *coccoliths* and *foraminifera*. The pure white chalks contain more than 90 per cent calcium cabonate. Chalks often contain nodules of flint or chert, together with large fossils. A common and well-studied example of a large fossil is the sea urchin *Micraster*.

CHALKS

Colour	white, grey or yellow
Mineralogy	mainly calcite, chalk is a very pure limestone containing little silt or mud; silica, present as flint or in marcasite, is common
Texture	fine-grained, finely porous, friable (crumbles easily) or compact
Structure	usually well bedded in thick extensive successions, with little small-scale bedding apparent; fossils usually present; flint and marcasite nodules common
Other tests	effervesces with and dissolves in dilute hydrochloric acid
Occurrence	chalks are pelagic limestones (made up of the skeletons of floating organisms) formed in shallow, open seas free from most other sediments; most are Cretaceous in origin but some are being formed today
Examples	the Weald (SE England), Antrim (Northern Ireland), France, Kansas (USA); recent chalks in the Black Sea; modern chalks are forming in Alpine lakes

Dolomites

Dolomites almost invariably began to form as lime deposits. At some stage, or stages, during their subsequent conversion into rock, the calcium carbonate was replaced by dolomite by reaction with magnesium-rich waters. Most limestones contain some magnesium carbonate. Geologists usually use the term dolomite only for rocks with a high proportion of the mineral dolomite. They are more abundant than those with magnesite as their main component. The process of dolomitization occurs either shortly after deposition of the sediment, or some time later when the rock is already well cemented. The process of conversion of calcite to dolomite involves a 12 per cent reduction in volume. This can result in a highly porous rock, which is commonly a reservoir rock for oil and natural gas. Dolomite (also known as magnesian limestone) is a source of magnesium oxide, which is used as an antacid and in insulating materials. Other uses of dolomite are as a refractory material and a building stone. Dolomite was named after the French mineralogist D. Dolomieu.

Dolomite

Dolomite

DOLOMITES

Colour	white, cream or grey, weathering to brown or pinkish
Mineralogy	a mixture of calcite and dolomite; magnesite may be present at high magnesium concentrations; lesser amounts of other detrital materials and cherts
Texture	coarse, medium or fine-grained; often compact but may be porous
Structure	often massive with any apparent bedding being on a large scale; concretions often present; fossil remains are usually destroyed by dolomitization; well jointed
Other tests	shows no obvious reaction to dilute hydrochloric acid, unlike limestones
Occurrence	mainly among other limestones and often in association with salt and gypsum deposits
Examples	NW Scotland (Sailmhor Formation), NE England (magnesian limestone); Saudi Arabia (Jurassic oil reservoir rocks); NE Italy; Bighorn, Wyoming and Niagara (USA)

Travertine and Tufa

Tufa

Tufa

Travertine and tufa are composed almost wholly of calcite. They are precipitated from water containing calcium carbonate in solution (as bicarbonate). Some form when water evaporates around springs or in caves. Others are created around geysers and hot springs by a change in temperature and/or the carbon dioxide content. Travertine is a quite compact rock, but tufa (or calc-tufa) is a porous, sponge-like rock. Travertine may be banded in various colours and shades due to staining by iron oxides. The dripstone deposits in caves give rise to the well-known features, stalactites and stalagmites.

Travertine marble

TRAVERTINE AND TUFA

Colour	white, cream or yellow, often stained brown to red
Mineralogy	predominantly calcite, stained to varying degrees by iron oxides
Texture	compact to earthy; crumbles easily
Structure	travertine may contain bands picked out in different amounts of iron oxide staining; stalactites and stalagmites show many small concentric 'growth rings'; some deposits around hot springs develop concentric and rounded (botryoidal) structures reminiscent of pisolitic limestones
Occurrence	found in limestone areas, in caves and around springs (hot or cold) and geysers
Examples	Auvergne (France), Tuscany and near Rome, especially around Tivoli (Italy), Dubois, Wyoming, and the Great Basin region in the western USA

Evaporites are chemical sediments formed by the precipitation of dissolved salts through the evaporation of water. Although gypsum and halite are the most common, evaporite deposits often contain other minerals in lesser amounts, including the potassium and magnesium salts sylvite, carnallite, polyhalite, kainite and kieserite. Evaporites are of great economic importance. They often form the cap rock in many oilfields. Their low density enables them to rise through other rocks – a process called *diapirism* – and form structural traps for oil and natural gas.

Daisy bed

Halite and polyhalite in clay

dolomitic clay matrix

Rock salt

EVAPORITES

Colour	colourless or white; variously coloured by impurities, often browns
Mineralogy	rock salt is essentially halite, with impurities of associated salts (carbonates and sulphates), clay minerals and iron oxides; rock gypsum is often associated with anhydrite, calcite, dolomite, clay minerals and iron oxides
Texture	massive, saccharoidal (sugary) or coarsely crystalline; gypsum may be fibrous, earthy or crumbly
Structure	may show bedding often strongly distorted; fossils rare; rock salt often in thick structureless beds with partings of shale; gypsum often interbedded with sandstone, mudstone or limestone
Occurrence	formed by the evaporation of salt-rich waters in lagoons, seas and lakes; gypsum may form by the action of water on anhydrite deposits
Examples	gypsum is common in the USA; alabaster in Italy, Iran and Pakistan; rock salt in England, Russia, NW Europe and Canada

Ironstones

Ironstone

fossil mould

Ironstone

Fossiliferous ironstone

Crudely bedded ironstone

fossils

Ironstones are a group of iron-rich sedimentary rocks. They are potential iron ores and have a characteristic rust-coloured appearance on weathering. Their origins and the nature of the iron-containing minerals present vary so widely that some people call them 'iron formations' rather than ironstones. Precambrian banded iron formations occur in old cratonic (shield) areas. They usually form thick sequences of iron minerals interbedded with cherts. Such ironstones are of great economic importance. Deposits from the Cambrian period onwards are usually thin and oolitic. The only iron deposits forming today are the bog iron ores of mid- to high-latitude lakes and swamps. Ironstones often contain fossils.

IRONSTONES

Colour	brown, red, green, yellow
Mineralogy	iron minerals present to give at least 15 per cent iron in the rock are commonly limonite, goethite, hematite, magnetite, pyrite, siderite, chamosite and glauconite; often cemented by calcite or dolomite
Texture	variable grain size and variable texture; sometimes oolitic
Structure	may be banded otherwise sedimentary structures common; fossils may be present
Occurrence	often interbedded with cherts, limestones and sandstones; ironstones themselves may also be classified as other sedimentary rocks (e.g. sandstones, limestones, shales)
Examples	large Precambrian iron-formations are in the Lake Superior region (North America) and the Hamersley Group of NW Australia; later ironstones in USA, Wales and England; modern freshwater bog ores are in Sweden and Finland

Cherts and Flints

C hert and flint are the traditional names for sedimentary chalcedony. However today, the term chert is preferred, while flint is used for a type of nodular chert occurring in chalk deposits. Cherts in the form of nodules occur most often in limestones and are often concentrated along one bedding plane. The silica in chalks comes from the remains of sponges, while, in deep-water limestones, it comes from radiolaria and diatoms (siliceous planktonic micro-organisms). Massive bedded cherts are formed from the skeletons of radiolaria and diatoms that are often deposited in deep water. The hardness of flint and its conchoidal fracture result in a sharp cutting edge, a property exploited by Stone Age people for making tools and weapons. For this reason care should be taken when handling cherts.

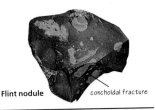

Flint nodule   conchoidal fracture

Banded chert

Flint tools

CHERTS AND FLINTS

Colour	blue-grey to almost black when nodular, weathering to a white powdery crust (patina); massive bedded cherts may be brown, green or black
Mineralogy	essentially silica as chalcedony
Texture	very fine-grained with smooth, conchoidal fracture
Structure	flint and chert form rounded nodules of varying forms; chert also forms massive thinly bedded deposits
Occurrence	nodules of flint and chert are often concentrated along the bedding planes of limestones and chalks; bedded radiolarian cherts form in lakes and marine areas with little other sedimentation
Examples	flint is found throughout Upper Cretaceous Chalk of W Europe, especially SE England; radiolarian cherts are found in Wales, Devon (England), Rhine Valley (Germany) and the Franciscan cherts of California and Oregon (USA); modern deposits of radiolarian ooze are found in the depths of the Indian and Pacific Oceans

Phosphatic Rocks

Phosphate-rich rocks, or phosphorites, form in seas where there is little sedimentation and where cold, nutrient-rich water wells up to the surface. The upwelling causes a high growth of phytoplankton and other surface organisms which can poison fish, causing mass mortalities. Because all organisms contain phosphates, especially in their bones, their remains produce phosphate-rich sediments. Smaller-scale phosphorites, formed from the skeletons of vertebrates, are called *bone beds* (*guano*). The excrement of sea birds (*guano*) can produce economically useful deposits for the fertilizer and chemical industries. They are insignificant geologically.

Polished slice of phosphorite

PHOSPHATIC ROCKS

Colour	white, yellow, brown, black
Mineralogy	complex phosphates of calcium, aluminium and iron; detrital sedimentary material usually present
Texture	fine- to coarse-grained when bedded; compact, earthy, granular, sometimes oolitic; guano is earthy and crumbles easily
Structure	bedded phosphate rocks mostly nodular with organic remains often replaced by phosphates; guano usually bedded
Occurrence	mainly associated with marine sediments, especially greensands, limestones and shales; guano, being the accumulated excrement of sea-birds, is associated with oceanic islands
Examples	phosphorites are found in Tennessee and California, and the Permian Phosphoria Formation of Idaho (USA); Ludlow Bone Bed and Rhaetic Bone Beds (SW England), Tertiary rocks of Algeria, Iraq, Morocco, Tunisia, Turkey and Western Sahara

Bone bed

bone fragments

Phosphorite

Carbonaceous Sediments

Anthracite

Peat

Bituminous coal

Lignite

CARBONACEOUS SEDIMENTS

Colour	light, brownish peat through to black coals
Mineralogy	peat is mainly vegetable remains; anthracite is almost pure carbon; coals may contain pyrite or other minerals
Texture	peat is felt-like and soft; lignite is like dried, woody peat; bituminous coals are hard and bright breaking into rectangular lumps; anthracite is shiny with conchoidal fracture
Structure	peat has little structure; bituminous hard coals usually have a distinctive bedding and prominent joint surfaces called *cleats*; fossil plant material may be visible on bedding planes
Occurrence	peat occurs in marshes and lakes in temperate and subarctic climates; most coals, as strata formed by the burial and alteration of woody material often alternating with sandstone and clay
Examples	peat bogs common in Ireland, Scotland, Poland, Canada; Carboniferous rocks of Europe and N America contain harder, older coals; soft brown coals occur in newer rocks in France and Germany

Carbonaceous sediments include peat and coal. Most coals are *humic* (formed from degraded wood), and some are *sapropelic* (formed from plant debris, spores and algae). Coals form a series with increasing carbon content, caused by increasing pressure and temperature on burial. The coals with the highest porportion of carbon are usually the oldest. *Lignite* or soft brown coals have a porous structure, resembling dried peat. Hard brown coals and *bituminous coals*, including household and coking coals, have an 85 to 90 per cent carbon content and contain volatiles, including hydrogen. *Steam coal* is hard and brittle. Shiny black *anthracite* is almost pure carbon, with a low content of volatile material.

Index

Index

Further reading and acknowledgements

Further Reading

Bauer, J., and Bouska, V., *Precious and Semiprecious Stones*. Octopus, London, 1983.

Blackburn, W.H. and Dennen, W.H., *Principles of Mineralogy*. Wm.C. Brown, Dubuque, Iowa, 1988.

Fry, N., *The Field Description of Metamorphic Rocks*, Geological Society of London Handbook Series. Open University Press, Milton Keynes, 1989.

Gribble, C.D. (Ed.), *Rutley's Elements of Mineralogy*, 27th edition. Unwin Hyman, London, 1988.

Hamilton, W.R., Woolley, A.R., and Bishop, A.C., *The Hamlyn Guide to Minerals, Rocks and Fossils*. Hamlyn, London, 1974.

Klein, C., and Hurlburt, C.S., *Manual of Mineralogy*, After J.D. Dana, 20th Edition. John Wiley and Sons, 1985.

Press, F., and Siever, R., *Earth*. Freeman and Company, New York, 1986.

Read, H.H., and Watson, J., *Introduction to Geology, Volume 1 Principles*. MacMillan Education Ltd., London, 1987.

Thorpe, R.S., and Brown, G., *The Field Description of Igneous Rocks*, Geological Society of London Handbook Series. Open University Press, Milton Keynes, 1990.

Tucker, M.E., *The Field Description of Sedimentary Rocks*, Geological Society of London Handbook Series. Open University Press, Milton Keynes, 1989.

Acknowledgements

The publishers wish to thank the following for kindly supplying photographs for this book: David Baker; Ron Boardman, Life Science Images; Peter Green, Imitor; Mike Grey; Natural History Museum, London; ZEFA.

The publishers wish to thank the following for providing specimens for photography: Professor M. Audley-Charles and Wendy Kirk of the University College of London; Daphne Kirk; Richard Taylor.

Colour photographs: Peter Green and Mike Grey